CHRIST IN ANCIENT VEDAS

CHRIST IN ANCIENT VEDAS

(An exciting, surprising and edifying discovery from the ancient Vedas, the sacred books of the Hindus, written between the period 2000 and 1200 B.C)

Dr. Joseph Padinjarekara M.A; M.A; M.T.S; ThD.

Scripture quotations, unless otherwise noted, are taken from the Holy Bible : New International Version. Copyright ©1984 International Bible Society. Used by permission of Zondervan Bible Publishers.

Cover Design by Timothy L. Kalata

Published in India:
India Mukti Mission
Pulickalkavala, Vazhoor, Kottayam 686 515
Kerala, India
For International Mukti Mission
Library of Congress Catalogue Card Number: 435300

For more information and permission for translation write to to International Mukti Mission, 283 Homewood Ave, Willowdale, ON. Canada M2R 2N6

ISBN: 1 -55011-202 -3

Welch Publishing Company Ltd.
960 The Gateway
Burlington, ON
L7K 5K7

Printed in Canada

O

GOD ALMIGHTY,

"ASATOMĀ SAT GAMAYA
TAMASOMĀ JYOTIRGAMAYA
MṚTYORMĀ AMṚTAM GAMAYA"

(FROM UNREAL LEAḌ ME TO THE REAL
FROM DARKNESS LEAD ME TO THE LIGHT
FROM DEATH LEAD ME TO IMMORTALITY.)

Bṛhadāraṇykopaniṣad 1:3:28.

DEDICATION

This book is humbly dedicated to all the
550 Million Hindus
who live in India,
Sri Lanka, Burma, Malaysia, Indonesia,
East and South Africa,
Fiji Islands, Trinidad and
all Caribbean countries,
England, U.S.A,
Canada and
other parts of the world.

ACKNOWLEDGEMENTS

Praise God. Now, here is the book, **Christ in Ancient Vedas** in your hand! I would like to remember some important people who helped me to bring out this precious truth in this century and the circumstances my Lord led me through. First of all, I praise God and thank Him for His guidance and support that I have experienced throughout this project.

The **Vedas** were written in Sanskrit, between the period 2000 and 1200 B.C. To the Hindus the Vedas are the sacred Scriptures and the final authority of their religion and philosophy. It is surprising to encounter the hidden Christ in the Vedas, the **Puruṣa-Prajāpati** (the Son of Man and the Lord of all) who gave Himself in sacrifice for the salvation of mankind.

It is not because of my ability or scholarship I could touch a subject like this. I am fully convinced of the grace of God which hovers over me ever since He put the seed of this theme in my mind and soul. As a baby grows in its mother's womb the theme has been developed in my mind as the days go by, even without my merit or effort. How marvelously and mysteriously the Lord has guided me through the path of sacrifice so that I could learn the mystery of sacrifice and the way of salvation from my Master's feet. All the glory and praise I bestowed upon the One who has loved me and gave His life for me on the cross.

I was not smart. My pre-university transcript was not good enough to go for medicine, engineering or any other scientific studies. Therefore, I ended up with Malayalam and Sanskrit Studies for my B.A. (Now, I thank God for my "smartlessness" which paved the way to study Sanskrit language. But I was not able to understand the wonderful plan of God in my life. I started to write novels and stories mostly about the painful experiences and failures of my own life which eventually led me to depression.) For my Master's degree too, I had no other choice but to continue the study of Malayalam and Sanskrit. (Now I remember with great respect all my teachers in the N.S.S. Hindu College, Changanachery and the University College, Trivandrum.)

Immediately after my graduation I was appointed as a lecturer in Sacred Heart College, Thevara, Cochin. I got a reputation from the society as a novelist but I could not stand before my conscience which reminded me always that I was a sinner. In fact, I was unhappy and depressed. All my novels and stories were telling my own sinful life. But I did not want to admit that sin was the basic problem of my depression. In 1970 December 19, I heard the good news of forgiveness of sins and salvation through the Lord Jesus Christ. I received Him as my personal Saviour. That incident changed my life completely. From there on I began to know: "In all things God works for the good of those who love Him, who have been called according to His purpose." (Romans 8:28)

As a Malayalam teacher I had no ambition to go outside Kerala State. But in 1973 the Lord brought me to Canada for his mysterious purpose. When I wanted to continue my studies in Canada I found that I had only one choice to register for the Master's degree in Sanskrit and Indian Studies in the University of Toronto. So I became a student in in1974.

However, I was not aware of the objectives of the Sanskrit studies. "Is it the will of the Lord?" Many times I have doubted. I quit all the programs of studies in 1975 when God called me for His work. Therefore I could not graduate in 1975. But the Lord told me not to give up Sanskrit studies and I continued without understanding the real purpose behind it.

From 1976 onwards I started to face many problems in the University. When I encountered severe problems one after another, again I started to doubt the credibility of the will of the Lord for my Sanskrit studies. On October 19, 1976, in a very critical moment, as I was coming from the fourteenth floor of the Roberts Library after my Sanskrit class I cried to the Lord and asked:

"Lord, What is the need of Sanskrit language for a Christian Evangelist?"

The Lord talked to me showing the following passage from the Bible.

"This is what the Sovereign Lord says:
'See I will beckon to the Gentiles, I will lift up the banner to the peoples; they will bring their sons in their arms and carry your daughters on their shoulders. . .Then you will know that I am the Lord; those who hope in Me will not be disappointed. . .I will contend with those who contend with you. . ." (Isaiah 49: 22-26)

Later on many a time the Lord has repeated the whole passage and that was enough for me to believe in Him and to know the need of Sanskrit for my profession. After that I have never doubted about the beneficial aspect of the study of Sanskrit language. The Lord has revealed to me His plan of evangelism from chapter 49 of Isaiah.

I continued my studies with great interest and much expectation for another year. But I had to wait four more years for my graduation. The Lord was preparing me to start research work for this book in those days. I was continuing my Sanskrit studies in the Toronto University until I was graduated in 1981. Meanwhile the Lord has given me opportunity to finish my theology courses in the Ontario Theological Seminary. (With gratitude I remember all my professors of the Toronto University and the Seminary.)

The original Sanskrit texts I have referred to are from the Roberts Library of the University of Toronto. Many thanks to the University for keeping thousands of Sanskrit texts in the library as precious gems. In the same way I remember with thanks the big library facility of the OTS and OBC where I could use those with complete freedom and Christian love. I appreciate the co-operation of the authors and publishers who kindly gave their permission to quote from their books. I have acknowledged every quote in the end-note and given a bibliography.

In 1980 I published my first booklet in this line entitled Christ Foreshadowed Ancient Vedas. Out of curiosity my Sanskrit professor read the book and responded: “Good and exciting truth. But many Hindus and Christians will not agree with you.” Of course, they have freedom to disagree with me. Since then I have been facing opposition and recognition as well. In 1988 I published some parts of this book in Malayalam entitled Mṛtyormā Amṛtam Gamaya. I was greatly encouraged by the wonderful responses written by Professor Mathew Ulakamthara and Dr. Narayanan Moosad of Kerala University. I remember them with gratitude. I thank God for my critics too. They are giving very good advertisement for my books free of cost. However, I am fully satisfied because the intellectuals are reading the book. When I see they are saved by the grace of God I forget everything.

My sincere gratitude goes to all the believers from different parts of the world praying for me and supporting me. Special thanks for Mukti Mission Church of God where I was pastoring from 1980 to 1989. I acknowledge your prayer support.

I was writing notes and collecting materials and scribbling here and there until I got a computer in 1988. (Thank God for the computer.) I had no idea about computer but my son taught me how to use it and thus I started actual writing part.

In 1990 February, when we moved from Toronto to Fort Erie we met a wonderful man of God, Rev. Arthur Pie who was a missionary in India for 15 years. He used his precious time to read this manuscript several times. I thank him for his corrections and valuable suggestions to this book. I also remember with gratitude brother Bill Chand and sister Ivy for their constant encouragement.

In 1986 I submitted the outline of this thesis to Canada Christian College for my doctoral program. It was approved by this fundamental and evangelical Christian College in June, 1990. I would like to thank in particular Dr. Mc Vetty and the faculty members of the College for approving my thesis to the level of doctorate degree in Theology.

I am grateful to Don Richardson for the beautiful and exciting Foreword of this book. Through his best selling books like Peace Child and Eternity in Their Hearts he has already established a good ground for Cross cultural evangelism. The time I have spent with him was precious and beneficial to my work.

Bro. Timothy L. Kalata , Buffalo NY, designed the attractive cover with much prayer and meditation. After donating this to the book he flew away to eternity at the presence of our Lord at the age of 26. I remember him with love.

Again my heartfelt thanks:

To Professor T. C. Mathew, Head of the Dept. of English, Govt. College, Kottayam who wrote a scholarly Exposition after he has studied the book carefully;

To Rev. P. A. V. Sam, the State Overseer of Church of God in India who wrote a letter of appreciation;

To George Kuruvilla Chavanikamannil, the President of Good News for India for his Preface of insight;

To Dr. Ezhamkulam Samkutty for his occasional phone calls and letters of encouragement and

To Rev. George John for his sincere evaluation of the book. They are all equally precious to me.

Many thanks to Dr. Ian Mc Phee and Welch Publishing Co.who publish this book in North America.

I would like to thank all my friends. My own dear brother Babu Padinjarekara is undertaking all the responsibilities of publishing this book in India. I ask my readers to pray for him and his family.

Finally I thank God for my wife, Ammini, and two children, Tom and Elizabeth. Days after days, nights after nights I was immersing in the ancient writings where Jesus was in its centre. Actually, I robbed their time. Willingly or not, they sacrificed many things. My dear wife always carried the heavy load of the family. Her sacrifice was great and without that the book would not have been written.

Most assuredly I can say I have written this book with sincere love. I have sacrificed many precious thing for this work. This whole book is the true story about the perfect sacrifice of a perfect **Man.**

Joseph Padinjarekara

CONTENTS

Introduction

PART I
THE MYSTERY OF SACRIFICE

Chapter 1

THE MAN SACRIFICE IN HEAVEN

Chapter 2

THE SACRIFICE CAME DOWN TO THE PLANET EARTH

Chapter 3

SACRIFICE- SHADOW AND SUBSTANCE

Chapter 4

JESUS -THE SACRIFICIAL LAMB

PART II

THE 10 CHARACTERISTICS AND THE RESULTS OF THE PRAJĀPATI- SACRIFICE FULFILLED IN JESUS' CRUCIFIXION AND RESURRECTION

Chapter 5

CHARACTERISTIC #1. THE NISKALANKA PURUṢA (THE SINLESS MAN)

Chapter 6

CHARACTERISTIC #2. THE CROWN OF THORNS

Chapter 7

CHARACTERISTIC #3. THE REJECTION

Chapter 8

CHARACTERISTIC #4. THE SILENT SUFFERER

Chapter 9

CHARACTERISTIC #5. CLOSE TO THE CROSS

Chapter 10

CHARACTERISTIC #6. THE BLOOD

Chapter 11

CHARACTERISTIC #7. THE BONES

Chapter 12

CHARACTERISTIC #8. THE MAN ALIVE!

Chapter 13

CHARACTERISTIC #9. THE FLESH OF THE MAN

Chapter 14

CHARACTERISTIC #10. TOTAL GIVING IN SACRIFICE AND THE OUTSTANDING RESULT

PART III

MUKTI- THE ULTIMATE RESULT OF SACRIFICE

Chapter 15

THE WAY OF MUKTI IN THE KATHOPANISAD

Chapter 16

PURUṢA - THE SUPREME GOAL (PARĀGATI) TO KNOW HIM IS IMMORTALITY

Chapter 17

KNOWING PURUṢA AS OUR GURU (MASTER)

Chapter 18

MANY WAYS AND THE ONE WAY

Chapter 19

THE MAN - PURUṢA - CHRIST JESUS - THE MEASURING ROD

PREFACE

God is unchanging. Eternally He remains the same. (See James 1:17). He has always loved the whole world; not just a few in the world, but the whole world.

His eternal desire is that all people know Him and His glory. (Malachi 1:11). This desire is supreme in His heart. He wants the whole earth to be full of the knowledge of His glory. (See Habakkuk 2:14).

We see this very clearly in the Old Testament which is the religious book of the Hebrews. There we see God choosing Abraham and the nation of Israel to carry out this purpose. He loved them and chose them as special people in order to be His ambassadors to the whole humanity.

His desire was to bless the whole world through Abraham and Israel. God said this to Abraham three times. (See Gen 12:1-3; 18:18; 22:18.). God even changed Abraham's original name to make sure he understood what God was trying to do. (His original name was Abram which in Hebrew means "exalted father"; God changed to Abraham which means "father of many nations.")

God repeated this revelation several times all through the Old Testament. (See Genesis 26:4,5; 28:14; 1. Kings 8:41-43; 2. Chronicles 6:32-33; Psalms 67; 96; 105; Isaiah 49:6; 51:4; 56:6-8; Zechariah 2:11)

Take Psalms 67 for example.

"May God be gracious to us and bless us
And cause His face to shine upon us
That Thy way may be known on the earth
Thy salvation among all nations.
.....God bless us
That all the ends of the earth may fear Him"

Why should God bless Israel? So that His way and His

salvation may be known among ALL NATIONS.

God is the one who created ALL NATIONS. He has no favorite nation. He loves the whole world and ALL people. ("For God so loved the WORLD that He gave His only begotten Son. . . John 3:16). **He wants all people everywhere to know Him and escape from eternal death and darkness.**

Because of His love for all the 'nations' (ethnic groups) He has revealed Himself to all ethnic groups. Don Richardson has masterfully shown this in his book, Eternity in Their Hearts. From time immemorial, God has left glimpses of His glory in the heart of almost every nation.

As time has passed this revelation of reality has become corrupted and clouded as it was mingled with man's own ideas of God. Yet here and there we see glimpses of eternal truth.

The concept of **Prajāpati Sacrifice** in Vedic literature is such a glimpse of truth. God in His mercy revealed long ago in the garden of Eden that man's sins can be covered only through the shedding of blood. God made a covenant with man who fell into sin that one day there would be a sacrifice by which Satan's strangle hold on humanity would be broken.

This truth is preserved in the concept of **Prajāpati Sacrifice.**

It is true that in Vedic writings we do see many other ideas, some even contradictory to that of an atoning sacrifice. That doesn't, however, diminish the value of this powerful redemptive analogy found in the ancient Hindu scriptures. Here is a precious gem which must receive much attention in the proclamation of the way of salvation in India.

I heartily comment this powerful book to all seekers of the truth. Through this work Dr. Joseph Padinjarekara has done an invaluable service to humanity. Read it and find the one who boldly asserted: "I am the way and the truth and the life. No one comes to God except through me." (John 14:6).

George Kuruvila Chavanikamannil M.A, M.Div.

FOREWORD

Years ago I read that Hinduism's most ancient text, the 3000- to 4000 year old **Ṛg Veda**, contains a prophecy about a "Lamb which must be sacrificed for the sins of mankind - a Lamb without blemish"! I thought it remarkable that the religion which now, more than any other major religion, emphasizes polytheism, idolatry and occult ritual, could possibly hold in any of its writings a truth so precious to Christians.

I viewed that one prophecy as a significant overruling of God. He had mercifully ordained that millions of idol-worshipping Hindus should have at least this one 'redemptive analogy,' i.e., a compass needle pointing them - from within their own culture - to our Judeo-Christian Scriptures and to Christ.

Little did I dream that, that prophecy was but one nugget evidencing a mother lode of similar typology viewing the **Ṛg Veda**. Not until I read this present monumental study by Dr. Joseph Padinjarekara did I learn that there are **scores** of Vedic foreshadowings of our Lord and many of them pre-date His advent by more than a millennium! How could this be?

My curiosity was aroused. I read more and more avidly. I learned that Vedic authors devoted the Supreme Deity as **Prajāpati** which means "the Lord of all creation." Yet **Prajāpati** is the very one who became **Puruṣa**, the sinless God-Man, so that as a man he who was also God could be offered as a sacrifice for mankind.

I was startled by this quotation from the **Upaniṣads:** "The one and only way to immortality is to know this **Puruṣa.** There is no other way to enter into eternal life." (chapter 1)

I read also: "The omnipotent, omnipresent and omniscient great God who is bigger than the universe limited Himself to just ten fingers (i.e., a small space) in **Puruṣa.**" (chapter 1) I read of "the **tree** whose roots are above and whose branches are below". (chapter 2). Out of my amazement I saw the **tree** and the **Puruṣa** are one and the same. This **tree** would be cut and, "as sap oozes from the cut **tree** so blood is being shed from the bruised **man.**" (chapters 2,10, etc.) I could go on, but it is better that you scale for yourself the mountain of evidence that Joseph Padinjarekara has amassed. His work is perhaps the deepest probe that any Christian has yet made to find a worthy bedrock long buried under the strata of subsequent less amenable developments in Hinduism, such as idolatry, caste, temple prostitution, suttee, etc.

Historically we Christians have tended to lapse into our own peculiar errors of nominalism and ritualism. Periodically we have needed prophets to lead us back to the Scriptural hub from which our many denominations spoked. For as the saying goes, "The further one gets from the hub, the more mud one finds clinging to the spokes!"

Perhaps thoughtful Hindus will find that Dr. Padinjarekara's ground breaking work will guide them back along their spokes to the Vedic hub of **their** wheel. If that happens, thoughtful Christians and those thoughtful Hindus may eventually discover to their mutual amazement that the Genesis 1 to 11 part of our hub and these crucial elements of the Vedic-hub are joined by a common axle - a shared influence from that ancient patriarchal monotheism that pre-dated both Judeo-Christianity and Hinduism.

California,
October 4, 1990. **DON RICHARDSON**

APPRECIATION

"I am very glad that Dr. Joseph Padinjarekara is bringing out a more detailed and informative book on Christ in Ancient Vedas. The author has made some indepth study on Ancient Vedic literature and his previous books in this line have been used of God to open the eyes of many Hindus to see Christ as the real **Prajāpati** (the Lord of all) who gave Himself in sacrifice which is also mentioned in the **Vedas.** I pray that this new book will be still more useful in pointing out Christ to all nations as the Saviour of the world.

May the Lord bless Bro. Padinjarekara in his sincere effort to present Christ to the people of India and to the Hindus all over the world across their religious and cultural background."

Rev. P. A. V. Sam
State Overseer, Church of God in India

EXPOSITION

Another exciting, edifying and enlightening literary piece from the desk of Dr. Joseph Padinjarekara. The author's literary career began as a secular novelist. His spiritual rebirth transformed him and his writings as well. Since then he has been catering to the spiritual needs of the readers in particular and mental and social needs in general.

'Christ in Ancient Vedas' is an inimitable work of its kind in content and in appearance. Undoubtedly it is the outcome of his indepth comparative religious studies of the Holy Bible and the Ancient Vedas of the East over a decade. To the readers, it must be surprising to note that the author has referred to many ancient Sanskrit texts as the part and parcel of his research.

The theme of the book is pivoted on the universal truth: *"God does not show favoritism but accepts men from every nation who fear Him and do what is right."* (Bible). God wants that the good news of salvation of human soul must be proclaimed among all nations, irrespective of caste, colour, or creed.

Indians are really fortunate of their rich ancient literary heritage in Sanskrit. By thorough study of these books Dr. Padinjarekara could unearth the precious gems from the depth and present them for display. The readers have the absolute freedom of impartially analyzing the pros and cons without any prejudice. It is fact that this work of art will quench the thirst of all those who are spiritually thirsty, especially the Easterners from the Vedic background.

The famous Indian Philosopher Swami Vivekananda thoroughly refutes the arguments of some extreme critics who brand Jesus Christ as a Westerner. He writes:

"Had I but lived in Palestine during the holy incarnation of the Lord Jesus Christ, I would have washed His holy feet not with my tears, but with blood of my heart. Jesus Christ was born in the Eastern world. Consequently the Easterners would comprehend well Him. . . Jesus Christ is not a stranger to us. He really belongs to the Eastern world which is ours. Only India of the East can really understand the **ahimsa dharma** (not injuring anybody, non violence) of Jesus Christ.

India can steadfastly follow the path of love chartered by Him and fulfill it. Jesus Christ is our heritage. . . **Tyāgis** (saints who rejected worldly pleasures) who live out the holy love of Jesus in their lives must rise up thousands of thousands. . . The **avatar** (incarnation) of love namely Jesus Christ must be proclaime by tom-tom in India, in towns, villages, and all over the land. . . Jesus Christ is our need. May He rule the hearts of the people of India." (From the books of Swami Vivekananda. C.L.S. Publication, India.)

'Christ in Ancient Vedas' will throw more light on the above statement of Swami Vivekananda.

Let me point out the importance of this work of Dr. Joseph Padinjarekara in one sentence: The book, **'Christ in Ancient Vedas'** is a milestone in the history of Cross Cultural Evangelism. The famous Indian Saint Sadhu Sunder Singh was quoted by John T. Seamands, Professor of Asbury Seminary while pointing out the significance of cross cultural evangelism:

"Sadhu. . ., the beloved Indian Christian, used to tell about a high caste Hindu in India who fainted from the summer heat while sitting on a train at railway station. Someone ran to the faucet, filled a cup with water, and brought it to the man in an attempt to revive him. But in spite of his condition the passenger would not accept the water because it was offered in the cup of a man belonging to another caste. Then someone noticed that the high caste man had a cup on the seat beside him; so he grabbed it, went out and filled it with water, returned and offered it to the man, who now readily accepted the water with gratitude.Then Sunder Singh would say to his audience, 'This is what I have been trying to say you missionaries from abroad. You have been offering the water of life to the people of India in a foreign cup, and we have been slow to receive it. If you will offer it in our cup (that is an indigenous form), we are much more likely to accept it." (Tell It Well: Communicating Gospel Across Cultures page 12. Beacon Hill Press of Kansas City.)

Dr. Billy Graham too emphasised the same truth at the World Congress on Evangelism: "We adapt our methods and terminology to the people to whom we are ministering. We can adapt certain illustrations or truths that will help a particular audience understand the gospel more clearly in the light of their cultural background."

The author unveils before the reader the ancient glory of

India. He introduces the mystic subject in very simple and lucid style. The reader cannot but keep close company with the author as a seeker of truth and thereby arises an inseparable bond between them. Both right and wrong kinds of sacrifices are discussed in the Introduction. The mystery of sacrifice portrayed in the opening pages of Part I, will no more be a mystery towards the end of it. But the curiosity of the reader is gradually aroused by the author's peculiar way of presentation.

Is it not exciting that the ten major characteristics of the **Prajāpati Sacrifice** portrayed in the Vedas as depicted in Part II of the book are literally fulfilled in the real **Prajāpati Sacrifice** of the Lord Jesus Christ, such as sinlessness, the separation, the rejection, the silent suffering, tying to the sacrificial pillar, the shed blood, unbroken bones, returning to life after sacrifice, eating the flesh of the sacrifice and the total giving in sacrifice!

In Part III of the book entitled **Mukti - the Ultimate Result of Sacrifice**, the author emerges as a psychologist cum philosopher and discuss the mystic unity of body, soul and spirit. The mystery of the life after death is clearly revealed in the story from the **Kaṭhopaniṣad**. The author accompanies the seeker from the simple to complex without letting the latter understands it. The chapter deals with the "many ways and the one way" is a eye opener to the seeker for he is convinced the four ways- **jñāna mārga, yoga mārga, karma mārga** and **bhakti marga** ultimately ends in one and the only way of salvation - the real **Prajāpati Sacrifice.**

The final chapter relieves the seeker from all confusions because he gets hold of the Measuring Rod which will be a new revelation to him.

May the Lord Almighty shower His manifold blessings upon the readers so that they could see the ultimate reality of sacrifice, know the **Puruṣa-Prajāpati** and inherit **mokṣa.**

Professor T. C. Mathew

INTRODUCTION

It may be a great surprise to some modern readers to discover the rich heritage of India and its vast literature in the Sanskrit language. But, as Will Durant writes in his book Our Oriental Heritage, "India has an impressive continuity of development and civilization from Mohanjodaro, 2900 B.C or earlier."[1]

The **Vedas** and the **Upaniṣads** are huge collections of precious books in Sanskrit, written before the Lord Jesus Christ's earthly ministry. "The **Upaniṣads** are the Himalayas of the soul," according to the scholars of the East and the West.[2] Climbing Mount Everest of the Himalayas is certainly a great event. It is very hard to make the ascent; but if someone brings us there bearing all the troubles and responsibilities, we will be delighted and excited.

World-renowned scholars like Max Muller spent their lifetime in the study of Vedic literature, faithfully attempting to understand and appreciate its greatness. In the Preface of the **Ṛg Veda Samhita** he wrote: "When I had written the last line of the **Ṛg Veda** and Sayana's commentary, and put down my pen, I felt as if I had parted with an old, old friend. For thirty years scarcely a day has passed on which my thoughts have not dwelt on this work, and for many a day, and many a night, too, the old poets of the Veda, and still more their orthodox and painstaking expositor, have been my never failing companions."[3]

The Vedas, the Upaniṣads, the Brāḥmaṇas and the Āraṇyakas

Indian literature begins with the **Vedas.** The hymns of the **Vedas** were preserved oral tradition for many centuries before they became concretized in the written form. Etymologically, **Veda** means knowledge, and more accurately, "supreme knowledge."It is called **'Braḥmavidya'** that can be interpreted as the knowledge of the way to **Braḥma** (God).

Vedic literature can be classified as:
(1) **Śruti (what is heard)**
(2) **Smriti (what is remembered or traditional.)**

The Vedas themselves come under four distinct categories:
(1) **The Ṛg Veda .**
(2) **The Yajur Veda.**
(3) **The Sāma Veda.**
(4) **The Atharva Veda.**
These four Vedas are under the category of **Śruti.**

The **Vedas** were written between the period of 2000 and 1200 B.C. Most scholars are unanimous about the date of the Vedas.

The **Atharva Veda** is rejected by some ancient scholars because the text contains the description of black magic and occultism. The sages of ancient times recognized only the first three **Vedas, the Vedatrayam** (the Three Vedas); the fourth was eliminated. The main theme of the **Vedas** is sacrifice.

The next group of the sacred texts is the **Brāhmaṇas** (1200-1000 B.C.) These writings explain the meaning and application of the **Vedic** hymns in relation to the performance of sacrifices.

The **Āraṇyakas** (1000.B.C) are the next group of literature. These books contain thoughts and meditations of the sages. The **Upaniṣads,** 'the Himalayas of the soul', were written between 1000 and 700 B.C. According to **Sriramakirishna Matham** publishers there are more than 120 published **Upaniṣads.**[4] But there are only 10 major **Upaniṣads** from **'Īśavāsyopaniṣad** to **Bṛhadāraṇyakopaniṣad'.**

Supernatural inspiration is claimed by the Vedic texts. Concerning the position of the Vedas Fr. Zacharias O.C.D writes:

"Hindu religious sects of the orthodox character as well as most of the philosophical schools, consider the Vedas not only as one of the earliest records of human thought so far available to us but also as the infallible guide and final authority both in religion and philosophy."[5] Swami Prabhavananda begins his book on the **Upaniṣads** as follows: "The oldest Scriptures of India, and the most important, are the Vedas. All orthodox Hindus recognize in them the origin of their faith and its highest written authority."[6]

The Quest for Salvation

These books represent a sincere search for God and a deeper quest for salvation. A well known prayer from the **Bṛhadāraṇyakopaniṣad,** written around 800 B.C., demonstrates the goal of their search:

"Asato mā sat gamaya

Tamaso mā jyotirgamaya

Mṛtyormā amṛtam gamaya"

("From the unreal lead me to the real
From darkness lead me to light
From death lead me to immortality.") [7]

Deliverance from all these - the unreal, darkness and death - is the basic need of every human being. It is a testament to the sincerity of these sages that they confessed that they were living in the shadow of vanity, darkness and death. They were seeking truth, light and eternal life. They could see these ahead but they knew that because they were mortal, the immortal gifts were beyond their reach. God is faithful to heed the groaning prayers of human beings. Who could say that God did not answer these men? God's revelation about light, truth and eternal life was given to us through the incarnation of God. When the Lord Jesus Christ was born into this world it was announced to the wise men of the East - the non-Jewish world. (Matthew 2)

I intend to show through the following pages that not only at His birth, but even before that, glimpses of the good news of salvation through the Lord Jesus Christ was revealed in the ancient **Vedas** and the **Upaniṣads**. We will see that when the ancients wrote about the sacrifices for attaining **Mokṣa** (eternal life) and the sacrifice of **Prajāpati** (Lord of All), they were quite unknowingly portraying the Lord Jesus Christ and His crucifixion as the way of salvation.

"**What is the ultimate goal of life?**" Raising this question Swami Nikhilananda gives us this answer: "It is the realization of freedom (**Mokṣa**), also called perfection, enlightenment, or immortality."[8] The Church fathers ask the same question in this way: "What is the chief end of man?" And here is their answer: "Man's chief end is to glorify God and to enjoy Him forever."[9] But being mortal and sinful, man is incapable of attaining immortality or (**Mokṣa**) by himself. That is why he is praying to be led from darkness to light. The word, "**Tamas**" is used in Sanskrit for "darkness". (**Tamasomā jyotirgamaya**). "Tamas" also means sin. Sin is the basic problem of mankind. Sin separated man from God.

According to the Hindu faith, a bath is a necessary preliminary to every religious act. Bathing is for purification. Before the morning bath the worshippers recite the following prayer which is commonly called the "**Prātasnāna mantram**":-

"I am a sinner.
What I have done is sin.
My soul is under sin.
I am the worst of the sinners.
Save me, O Lord of the Sacrifice."[10]

Everyday they repeat the same prayer and confess that they are sinners and proclaim that mere water cannot wash away the sin of the inner man. Macbeth, the tragic hero of the Shakespearean drama, kills Duncan and after that begins to wash the blood spots with water. But he says, "Will all great Neptune's ocean wash this blood clean from my hand?"[11] Macbeth, through his crime, had stumbled on a profound spiritual truth: the guilt of sin cannot be washed away by water. For the remission of sin something more powerful, a very deep acting detergent, a divine and living cleanser is needed. For forgiveness of sins and to obtain **Mokṣa** or **Mukti** (salvation), the Vedas suggest following the path of sacrifice (**Yajña**).

The Proper and Improper Sacrifices

The concept of sacrifice is deeply rooted and grounded in the human heart from the creation of the world. **Sacrifice** is the most favoured word for almost all types of people: literary men, politicians, doctors, engineers, true worshippers of God and even the occult. The word 'sacrifice' originally indicated an act of making an offering to God in worship or atonement. The dictionary gives us more meanings. These include giving up of some cherished or desired object, person, idea and so on for the sake of something else which is of greater value. The great novelist, Tolstoy, sacrificed his life for literature. Mahatma Gandhi sacrificed his life for the nation. But from the beginning there had been right and proper sacrifices acceptable to God as well as improper sacrifices which were not acceptable. In the Bible we see that the sacrifice of Abel was accepted by God, Cain's offering was rejected (Genesis 4:5).

Reports of Human Sacrifices in our Cities

It is surprising to see that in this twentieth century some people in our modern cities are performing animal sacrifices and even human sacrifices. As Jerry Johnston writes in his book, "Thousands of children from neighborhoods, preschools and daycare centres around the country are telling strikingly similar stories of human and animal sacrifices in connection with strange devil rituals."[12] Terrible stories of human sacrifice done by the so-called civilized people of North American continent are described in his book, <u>The Edge of Evil - The Rise of Satanism in North America.</u> A teen age boy named Sean Sellers killed his parents to please his master satan and for him that murder was a sacrifice. He is the youngest man on death row in Oklahoma state penitentiary where he was interviewed by Jerry Johnston, the author of the book. When he was asked why he killed them the boy replied, "Because I loved them."[13] The boy was sacrificing his best to his master.

In this context, the modern reader has considerable difficulty in believing the doctrine of sacrifice for salvation. Therefore the right and wrong kinds of sacrifices have to be determined on the basis of the revelation of God. Sacrifice is often considered the highest form of worship and adoration without which there is no worship. It is written in the Holy Bible, "Worship the Lord your God, and serve Him only." (Matthew 4:10) God alone is worthy to be worshipped. Therefore what does the Scripture say? Do we need to sacrifice animals or human beings for obtaining salvation? What does sacrifice mean according to the Vedas and the Upanisads? What is the teaching of Jesus Christ concerning sacrifice?

My goal is to find answers to these very important questions from the Vedic literature and the Holy Bible. In the following chapters I will try to show that there is a thread of teachings in Vedic literature which clearly points to Christ as its fulfillment.

PART I

THE MYSTERY OF SACRIFICE

Chapter 1

THE MAN-SACRIFICE IN HEAVEN

The Vedas and Sacrifices

Sacrifice plays a vital role in Vedic literature. The **Ṛg Veda** says: "The sacrifice is extended in all directions by means of its threads."[14] In another place, it is written that the sacrifice is the navel of the world.[15] Why is sacrifice so important? Why is sacrifice awarded such a central role in the life of a man? The Vedas proclaim that sacrifice is the way to attain heaven and the remission of sin. (This will be discussed later.) In the **Kaṭhopaniṣad**, the famous Hindu text written before Christ, we read, "the sacrifice which leads to heaven is how the heaven seekers attain eternal life."[16] The importance of this sacrifice is emphasized when Naciketa, the protagonist of this text, says, "I indeed know that fire sacrifice leads to heaven and is the way to attain heaven."[17] In the **Śathapathabrāḥmaṇa,** another sacred book of the Hindus written before Christ, we read: "By means of sacrifice the gods attained that supreme authority which they now wield."[18] Who are these gods? Were they sinful? We have to look into these subjects more closely later but now I want to just point out that there are countless references in Vedic literature to the importance of sacrifice in connection with attaining immortality.[19]

The ancient sages say:

"Rta (sacrifice) alone is the highest (form of worship); no one goes beyond rta." [20]

THE SUPREME SACRIFICE IN THE VEDAS

The Vedas say that the proper kind of sacrifice on earth is the symbolic representation of a perfect sacrifice of God performed in heaven. That is the supreme sacrifice which is the model for all other sacrifices. (We have to note the place and the time of the sacrifice. We will see this later.)

In the seventh chapter of the second khanda of the **Tāṇdyamahābrāḥmaṇa,** the following verse describes a supreme sacrifice (Yajña) of the supreme God:

"Prajāpatirddevebhyāṃ ātmānaṃ

Yajñaṃ kṛtvā prāyacchat."

("Having done a self-sacrifice Prajāpati offered Himself for the gods.")

The supreme God is also known as **Prajāpati** in Vedic literature. The literal meaning of **Prajāpati** is the Lord of **praja** which can be interpreted as the **Lord of all** creation. (In Hindu mythology - including some parts of the Vedas - we may see characters named 'prajāpati' as we can read in Puranic Encylopedia. But they are not related to the true and original **Prajāpati** who is the Lord of all creation.)

Usually He receives offerings and sacrifices. But here, the sacrifice of **Prajāpati** is significant because the victim of the sacrifice is God Himself. The **Ṛg Veda** says, *"The actual sacrifice is Prajāpati Himself."* [21] The translation by H. Aguilar, a Sanskrit scholar, of the verses of the **Śatapathabrāḥmaṇa** gives more details about the supreme sacrifice: "And indeed, there was no other (victim) meet for sacrifice but that one (**Prajāpati**), and the gods set about offering him up in sacrifice. Wherefore it is with reference to this that **Ṛsi** has said: 'The gods offered up the sacrifice with the help of the sacrifice - for with the help of the sacrifice they did offer up him (Prajāpati), the sacrifice: - these were the first ordinances, for these laws were instituted first.' "[22]

Who Offered Himself in a Sacrifice?

In the **Ṛg Veda**, the famous chapter of the **Puruṣasūkta** deals with the divine and human aspects of Prajāpati and His sacrifice.[23] We have an extensive study of sacrifice in the Brāḥmaṇa Texts. The **Māddhyandinīya Śathapathabrāhmaṇa** says that **Puruṣa** and **Prajāpati** are one and the same person (**Puruṣohi Prajāpati**).[24] Here Prajāpati is called **Puruṣa** which means **Man**. This Man is not an ordinary human being and yet He is called Man. The greatness of Puruṣa is made clear in the **Kaṭhopaniṣad**:

"Puruṣa is superior to everything. Nothing is superior to Puruṣa. He is the end and the highest goal." (. . .Avyaktāt Puruṣah paraḥ. Puruṣānna paraṃ kincitsā kāṣthā sā parā gati.)[25]

Again the **Kaṭhopaniṣad** says,

"And verily beyond the unmanifest is the supreme Puruṣa, . . . ***One who knows Him becomes free and attains immortality."***
("Avyaktātu paraḥ Puruṣo. . . yajñātva mucyate janturamṛtatvaṃ ca gacchati.")[26]

This Puruṣa is the perfect victim for the one great sacrifice, performed even before the creation of the world. This is the main theme of the **Ṛg Vedic Puruṣasūkta** where we read the sacrifice of **Puruṣa/Prajāpati** which will be portrayed in detail. It is very important for us to know this **Puruṣa (Man)** for our salvation. The **Śvetāśvataropaniṣad says that the one and the only way to immortality is to know this Puruṣa and there is no other way to enter into eternal life. (". . .Nānyaḥpanthā vidyate - ayanāya".)** [27]

Seeing this **Puruṣa**, H. Aguilar writes in his book, The Sacrifice in the Ṛgveda, as follows:

"To me the myth of **Puruṣa/Prajāpati** is qualitatively different from more or less similar myths that are found in the Mythologies of the Pacific Islands or of China or in Germanic tradition which lack the complexity of relations that the Indian myth has with the entire Vedic doctrine of sacrifice and with the Upanishadic conception of **ātma/brahma**. Taken in its totality the myth of **Puruṣa/Prajāpati** is not unworthy of the Christian conception of the redemptive incarnation of the **Logos** (Word = Jesus) by means of **"Kenosis"** leaving out the question as to whether they (Christians) can be homologated (in agreement) or not."[28]

H. Aguilar's impartial argument brings us to this important conclusion: the supreme sacrifice of Vedic literature is strikingly compatible with the Christian notion of sacrifice which finds its highest expression in the crucifixion of Christ.

Jesus Christ - The Son of Man (Puruṣa)

When we come to the New Testament we can see that the Lord Jesus Christ refers to Himself as 'Son of Man' almost all the time even though He is the Son of God. Jesus asked His disciples,

"'Who do people say the Son of Man is?'

They replied, 'Some say John the Baptist; others say Elijah; and still others Jeremiah or one of the prophets.'

'But what about you?' He asked. 'Who do you say I am?'

Simon Peter answered, 'You are the Christ, the Son of the living God.'" (Matthew 16:13-16)

On the mountain top, at the time of His transfiguration, the disciples heard the voice of God from heaven concerning Jesus: "This is my Son, whom I love; with Him I am well pleased. Listen to Him." (Matthew 17:5). But in the next moment Jesus called Himself 'the Son of Man'. "As they were coming down from the mountain, Jesus instructed them, 'Don't tell anyone what you have seen, until the **Son of MAN** has been raised from the dead.' "(v.9)

Whenever Jesus spoke of His mission, His sacrificial death, He used the term, **Son of Man** as we read in Matthew 20:28: *"Just as the Son of Man did not come to be served, but to serve and give His life as a ransom for many."* Daniel could see this Son of Man in his vision in the Old Testament: "In my vision at night I looked, and there before me was one like a Son of Man, coming with the clouds of heaven." (Daniel 7:13) Jesus Christ quoted the same verse about Himself to the high priests as the answer to their question: *"But I say to all of you: In future you will see the Son of Man sitting at the right hand of the Mighty One and coming on the clouds of heaven." (Matthew* 26:64.)

Jesus officially used this title, **the Son of Man,** a concept very similar to **Puruṣa**, when He came to this world to fulfill His mission. Leon Morris, a famous theologian and author of this century, explains this idea as follows: "He had come to fulfill all that the Son of Man implies. . . If we seek to find out what this involves we naturally turn to the Old Testament. There the expression is found in some Psalms and in the book of Ezekiel as a synonym for 'man'. . .'The Son of Man' was, so to speak, His official title. It was the way He described Himself in the light of His mission. He came to be the glorious Son of Man. But the passages show that He would reach His true glory precisely by suffering."29 In other words, the majesty of this Man reaches its climax in His sacrifice. Here we have to note the meaning of **Puruṣa** is Man.

The Man-Sacrifice in the Puruṣasūkta

Puruṣasūkta is considered the heart of the **Ṛg Veda.** The Ninetieth chapter of the tenth **mandala** of the **Ṛg Veda** deals with the sacrifice of the sinless, perfect and omnipotent **Puruṣa** in sixteen majestic verses. (We can also find the portions of the **Puruṣasūkta** in the**Sāma, Yajur** and **Atharva Vedas**).

According to the Vedas all creation is the result of this sacrifice and this is the way to obtain heaven. (It is explained later). This is the earliest established principle. The Sanskrit Department of Kerala University, India, has given a prominent place to the **Puruṣasūkta** in their syllabus for the graduate program. Traditional Hinduism always places much importance on this portion of the **Vedas.** All the **Pūjas** and other religious ceremonies must begin by reciting the verses of the **Puruṣasūkta.**[30]

The content of the **Puruṣasūkta** can be divided into two parts:

(1) The majesty of the Puruṣa.
(2) The sacrifice of the Puruṣa.

The Majesty of the Puruṣa

The first few verses are devoted to an explanation of the majesty of the glorious Puruṣa.

Let us see the first verse:

"Sahasraśīrṣā-Puruṣaḥ

sahasrākṣaḥ sahsrapāt

sa bhūmim viśvato vṛtvā-

atyatiṣṭhaddaśāngulaṃ."

{Puruṣa has a thousand heads, a thousand eyes and a thousand feet. Encompassing earth on all sides, He rules. And He limited Himself to ten angulas (fingers).} {And He "was over and above by ten angulas (fingers)."} 31

This extraordinary Man (**Puruṣa**) is introduced in a supernatural way. The Man has a thousand heads, thousand eyes, a thousand feet. Encompassing earth on all sides He shines. The Man knows everything because He has a thousand heads and sees everything since He has a thousand eyes and can go anywhere with His thousand feet. It almost resembles the vision of the glory of God depicted in the tenth chapter of the book of Ezekiel in the Holy Bible. The **cherubim,** the embodiment of the glory of God that the prophet Ezekiel saw, can go everywhere without turning since the cherubim have many eyes. The verse says, "Their (cherubim's) entire bodies, including their backs, their hands and their wings were completely full of eyes, as were their four wheels." (Ezekiel 10:12). Ezekiel could see many eyes that he could not even count. In the same way the sage who wrote the **Puruṣasūkta** saw a thousand eyes of the **Puruṣa**. This does not mean that the **Ṛsi** could count the exact number of the eyes. Nalappat Narayana Menon, one of the Sanskrit scholars of South India, used the word, `countless' instead of the word,`thousand' when he translated the first hymn of the **Puruṣasūkta.**[32]

An authentic study about **Puruṣasūkta** by N. J. Shende is published by the Centre of advanced study in Sanskrit in the University of Poona, India. In this study the author specifies the following important points:

(1) "The Creator is Puruṣa (endowed with a human form)."
(2) "Puruṣa is Īśāna or Īśvara (Almighty God). He is the Lord of gods and of the whole universe. He is all-prevading." [33]

The divinity and the humanity of **Puruṣa** are very clear in the text.

The Vedic sages are not portraying a literal man who has a thousand heads, a thousand eyes etc. (If those were literal the Man should have two thousand eyes instead of one thousand). The verse simply describes the attributes of omnipresence, the omniscience and the omnipotence. These attributes are normally ascribed to God. However, in the **Puruṣasūkta** these qualities are seen in a Man. How can this be? Such a paradox was fulfilled when God came down on earth as a Man. Seeing Jesus as the incarnated God St. Paul writes: "He is the image of the invisible God." (Colossians 1:15) In the book of Hebrews it is written about Him, "He is the exact representation of God's nature." (Hebrews 1:2) The opening verses of the Gospel of John beautifully present the incarnation of God: *"In the beginning was the Word, and the Word was with God and the Word was God.... The Word became flesh and made His dwelling among us. We have seen His glory, the glory of the One and the Only, who came from the Father, full of grace and truth."* (John 1:1,14)

The Almighty God is holy and sinless. This refers to His nature which will never change. We can see this nature in Jesus, in whom there was no sin, just as in the dream of the **Ṛsis** about **'Niṣkalanka Puruṣa', the sinless Man.**

The Concept of Daśāngulaṃ (Ten Fingers)

The first verse ends with this obscure statement: **"Atyatiṣṭhaddaśāngulaṃ".** Vaman Shivram Apte quotes this portion of the **Ṛg Veda** in his Sanskrit English Dictionary under the word **aṭiṣtha** which means to excel. Depending on this meaning he translates the above quoted statement as follows: "was over and above by ten **angulas** (fingers.)"[34] Dr. M. Dhavamony follows him and translates the verse more or less the same way: "He **(Puruṣa)** extended beyond it the length of the ten fingers."[35] A well known Malayalam poet of South India, Vallathol, also translates the portion in the same way.[36] Another Malayalam poet and Sanskrit scholar Nalappat Narayana Menon, did not bother to touch the word **'daśāngulaṃ'** when he translated the portion in his book.[37]

Angulaḥ means a finger or the thumb. Twenty four **angulas** make one cubit. So the length of ten **angulas** is very little. What is the significance in this concept in which we see the **Man** to be over and above by only 10 fingers? Can we set a limit to the greatness of God? If we take this interpretation we have to say the greatness of God is equal to all this universe plus ten fingers. However it is not right to say that the greatness of God is limited and it is also quite contrary to the spirit of the **Puruṣasūkta.** The scholars interpret the verse on the basis of the word **'atiṣtha'**(to excel). But this word differs in meaning according to the context. Sayanacarya, who wrote the commentary on the **Puruṣasūkta** in Sanskrit has given us the key to the secret when he used the word **'daśāngulaparimitaṃ'** which means limited up to the ten fingers.[38] Who limited himself up to ten fingers? The answer is very clear from the context. He is none other than **Puruṣa** because the one and the only person in this verse is **Puruṣa.** Now note the beauty of the verse:

> *The omnipotent, omnipresent and omniscient great God who is bigger than the universe limited Himself to just ten fingers in* ***Puruṣa.***

(Man has ten fingers! And also ten fingers suggest how much the great personality of God shrinks in a man.) This is an exciting and great story which deserves universal attention. In the first verse of the **Puruṣasūkta** itself we can see the most important theme of the whole **suktas.** Borrowing the terminology of the Holy Bible we can say: The Almighty God humbled and emptied Himself as a Man. This is the greatest news which must be proclaimed all over the world.

The majestic description of the **Puruṣa** is continued in the next verse:

> **"Puruṣa evedam sarvaṃ**
>
> **yadbhūtaṃ yacca bhavyaṃ**
>
> **utāmṛtatvasyeśāno**
>
> **yadannenātirohati."**

("Puruṣa is all this universe, what has been and what will be. And He is the Lord of immortality, which He provides without food [natural substance].") [39]

What a great glory is revealed here! This Man is superior to the universe and even to time itself. He is the Lord of immortality. He is the beginning and the end. The Lord God says in the book of Revelation, "*I am the Alpha and the Omega, who is and who was, and who is to come, the Almighty.*" (Revelation 1:8) It is obvious that this refers to the Lord Jesus Christ.

Puruṣa is the Lord of immortality or eternal life. Jesus says, "For I have come down from heaven not to do my will but to do the will of Him who sent Me. . . that I shall lose none of all that He has given Me, but RAISE them up at the last day. For My Father's will is that everyone who looks to the Son and believes **in Him shall have eternal life, and I will raise him up at the last day."** (John 6:38-40) Before Jesus raised Lazarus from the dead, He publicly said to Martha, "I am the resurrection and the life. He who believes in Me will live, even though he dies;and whoever lives and believes in Me will never die."(John 11:25)

This teaching of Jesus Christ was questioned by the Jews and they ridiculed Him, by calling Him a Samaritan and demon possessed. In answer to this Jesus said:

"I tell you the truth, if anyone keeps My word, he will never see death." (John 8:51)

"At this the Jews exclaimed,

'Now we know you are demon-possessed! Abraham died and so did the prophets, yet you say that if anyone keeps your word, he will never taste death. Are you greater than our father Abraham? He died and so did the prophets. Who do you think you are?'

Jesus replied,'If I glorify myself, my glory means nothing. My Father, who you claim as your God, is the one who glorifies me. Though you do not know Him, I know Him. . .Your father Abraham rejoiced at the thought of seeing my day. He saw it and was glad.'

'You are not yet fifty years old,' the Jews said to Him,'and you have seen Abraham!'

'I tell you the truth,' Jesus answered, **'before Abraham was born, I am!'** At this, they picked up stones to stone Him, but Jesus hid Himself, slipped away from the temple grounds." (John 8:52-58)

Even though the great glory of God was revealed in bodily form in their presence, most of them did not want to believe in Him. It was because of their attitude toward the truth. When Jesus raised Lazarus from the dead before a multitude of Jewish people, was He not proving His statement claiming that He is the Lord of immortality?

They saw Lazarus, whom Jesus had raised from the dead but instead of believing in Him, "they made plans to kill Lazarus as well." (John 12:10) They did not believe the truth because they were not truth-seekers. The truth came to this world in flesh for the people who really seek for truth. Jesus said, *"I am the truth."* (John 14:6) *To Pilate Jesus said, "I came to this world to testify to the truth. Everyone on the side of truth listens to me."* (John 18:37) We can see this truth in the **Puruṣasūkta** where we read that the **Puruṣa** is the Lord of immortality. This is completely fulfilled in Jesus. He established the truth by giving life to numerous people and by His own sacrificial death and His glorious resurrection.

Before we go to the description of the Man-Sacrifice in the **Puruṣasūkta** let us go through two more verses which deal with the majesty and the incarnation of this **Man.**

Quoting verses 3 and 4 together:

"Etāvānasya mahima-ato

jyāyāmśca Pūruṣaḥ

pādo-asya viśva bhūtāni

tripādasyāmṛtaṃ divi.

Tripadūrdhva udaitpuruṣaḥ

pādou-asyehā bhavatpunaḥ

tato viṣvaṅvykrāmat

sāśanānaśane abhi."

(This [creation] is the glory of the Puruṣa. - So great is His majesty -. Still He is greater than this [creation]. One fourth of [the personality of] the Puruṣa is in the world. Three fourths of Him are still living eternally in heaven.

Puruṣa arose upwards with three quarters of Himself. One

quarter of Him was born here. From that [quarter of His glorious personality] He spread [life] in all living beings.)

From these verses we have to note that only a part of His greatness is manifested on this earth. "One fourth of **Puruṣa** is in the world." When God came down on this planet earth, He manifested only a part of His glory. The verse says, "three fourths of Him are still living eternally in heaven." The same idea is communicated through the next verse: "Puruṣa rose upwards with three quarters of Himself." When God came to earth as a man, He was limited by His humanity as symbolically suggested by the expression 'the ten fingers' as we have seen in the first **sūkta.** St. Paul wrote in the book of Philippians as follows:

"Christ Jesus: Who being in the very nature of God, did not consider equality with God something to be grasped, but made Himself nothing,t taking the very nature of a servant, being made in human likeness. And being found in appearance as a MAN. . ." (Philippians 2:6-8) Even though Jesus Christ is the image of the invisible God, He is the mystery of God. St. Paul refers to this mystery, Christ, *"in whom are hidden all the treasures of wisdom and knowledge."* (Colossians 2:3)

The full glory of God was hidden in this Man in His earthly body. His glory is revealed to the people who seek Him. On one occasion on the mountain top He was transfigured before Peter, John and James. "His face shone like the sun, and His clothes became as white as light. Just then there appeared before them Moses and Elijah, talking with Jesus. . . While He was still speaking, a bright cloud enveloped them, and a voice from the cloud said, 'This is my Son, whom I love;with Him I am well pleased. Listen to Him.' " (Matthew 17:2-5) That is the reason why Peter could write as follows: "We did not follow cleverly invented stories when we told you about the power and coming of our Lord Jesus Christ, but we were eyewitnesses of His majesty. For He received honour and glory from God the Father when the voice came to Him from the Majestic Glory, saying, 'This is my Son, whom I love; with Him I am well pleased.' We ourselves heard this voice that came from heaven when we were with Him on the sacred mountain." (2 Peter 1:16-18)

The Sacrifice of the Puruṣa

This glorious Man is offered as the perfect sacrifice. Even though He was the omnipotent and mighty God He was bound as the sacrificial animal and was offered. In other words He gave Himself in the sacrifice as we have seen in the **Tāṇdyamahābrāḥmaṇa.** (Having done a self-sacrifice, **Prajāpati** offered Himself. . .)[40] That is the main theme of the **Puruṣasūkta.** Thus we read from the text:

"Yatpuruṣeṇa haviṣā devā

yajñamatanvata

vasanto asya-āsīdājyaṃ

grīṣma idhmaḥ śaraddhaviḥ.

Taṃ yajñaṃ barhiṣi

praukṣanpuruṣaṃ jātamagrataḥ

tena devā ayajanta

sādhyā ṛṣayaśca ye."

(When the gods performed a sacrifice with Puruṣa as an oblation, spring was its melted butter, summer its fuel, and autumn its oblation. They sprinkled Puruṣa, born in the beginning, as a sacrifice in the straw. The gods, the sādhyas and the seers sacrificed Him as the victim.) [41]

Puruṣa is the sacrificial victim. Seers and gods are the sacrificers. This central idea is very clear in these verses even though all other expressions need further explanation. We will see who these seers and gods are later. There is no doubt that "the sacrifice, blessed on the straw was the **Man** born in the beginning. Gods sacrificed by means of Him; so did the seers and the saints."[42]

Creation of the World - The Primary Result of the Man-Sacrifice

The following verses in the **Puruṣasūkta** show clearly that the sacrifice was an act of total giving (**"Tasmādyajñātsarvahutaḥ. . . .**)[43] The results of the act of total giving are narrated through verses 5 and 8 to 15. This will be explained in detail in chapter 14 dealing with the results of the supreme sacrifice. But in short, we can say, in the light of verses from **the Puruṣasūkta,** *that the universe was created by the sacrifice of the Puruṣa.* Let us quote the 5th verse in this context:

"Tasmādvirālajāyata

virājo adhipūruṣaḥ

sa jāto atyaricyata

paśćādbhūmimadho puraḥ"

{From that (from a part of Puruṣa) the universe (virāj) was born and that was made the seat of Puruṣa and He became omnipresent.}

The first five verses in the **Puruṣasūkta** are about the majesty of the **Puruṣa.** Whatever is created in this world was created by **Puruṣa** and here He sits enthroned with His presence filling the whole earth. Thus He is known as **Virāt-Puruṣa.** The creation of the universe is the primary result of the **Man's** sacrifice in heaven. Even though we see the sacrifice from verse 6 onwards the author of the text mentions the primary result of the sacrifice in verse 5. Verse 13 clearly says that the sun, the moon, the fire and the wind were created as the result of this sacrifice:

"Candramā manaso jāta-

śćakṣoḥsūryo ajāyata

mukhādindraśćagniśća

prāṇādvāyurajāyata."

(The moon was born from His mind. The sun came out from His eye. Indra (lightning, rain) and fire were produced from His mouth. From His breath the wind was born.)

Thus through the Puruṣa everything was created. St. John writes about Jesus in the same way: *"Through Him (Jesus) all things were made; without Him nothing was made that has been made." (John 1:3) St. Paul in the book of Romans exalts Him, "For from Him and through Him and to Him are all things. To Him be the glory for ever!"* (Romans 11:36) In the first chapter of the book of Hebrews where the author deals with the supremacy of Christ, it is clear that **Man Jesus** who laid the foundations of the earth in the beginning. Read the following verses carefully:

"And again, when God brings His firstborn into the world, He says,
'Let all God's angels worship Him." (Hebrews 1:6)

"About the Son He (God) says,
*'Your throne, **O God**, will last forever. . . "* (v.8)

"He (God) also says,
'In the beginning, O Lord, You laid the foundations of the earth, and the heavens are the work of Your hands. They will perish, but you remain;. . . " (verses 10 & 11)

See! God, the heavenly Father, addressed the Son, the Man Christ Jesus, as "O God," and acknowledged that He laid the foundations of the world and created the heavens.

Through this Puruṣa all things were made and He created everything else by His sacrifice. As we have seen above from hymn number 3, "Puruṣa spread life in all living beings from the quarter of His glorious personality which appeared on this earth. See what a profound truth this is that we have just discovered in the Ṛg Vedic Puruṣasūkta.

In the light of the truth we have found in the portions of the Scriptures quoted above, we encounter some more precious information concerning the perfect sacrifice of **Prajāpati.**

(1) The Place of the Sacrifice

Where is the actual place of this sacrifice? As the earth was the result of the sacrifice it could not have happened on this earth. The earth was not yet created when the perfect **Puruṣa/Prajāpati's** sacrifice was performed. Then, where was the altar of the supreme sacrifice? It is where the Almighty God, the **Puruṣa/Prajāpati,** dwells. This is the simplest and clearest answer. We call the place heaven. God gave a glimpse of heaven to St. John in the book of Revelation. There He is seen *as a "a Lamb, looking as if it had been slain, standing in the centre of the throne of God"*. (Revelation 5: 6) That sacrificial Lamb is referred to as Jesus Christ who had been crucified. This subject has to be treated later in detail.

(2) The Time of the Sacrifice

When did the sacrifice of **Puruṣa** occur? From the creation of the world is the one and the only answer that we can discover from the **Puruṣasūkta.** *The Holy Bible says the same thing about the sacrifice of Jesus: "the Lamb that was slain from the creation of the world."* (Revelation 13: 8)

The Pre-existence of Jesus Christ

Christ was born in Bethlehem nearly 2000 years ago. But about His pre-existence we have many verses in the Scriptures, both in the Old Testament and the New Testament. When Micah predicts Christ's birth-place in 750 B.C he also points out His pre-existence: *"But you, Bethlehem Ephrathah, though you are small among the clans of Judah, out of you will come for me one who will be ruler over Israel, whose origins are from old, from ancient times."* (Micah 5: 2) According to this prophecy the Jewish nation was expecting their Messiah the King. The chief priests and the teachers of the law were aware of this prophecy. They could easily read the prophetical passage to King Herod when they were asked the place of birth of the Messiah.[44] They were expecting their Messiah who would be the king of their nation like King David. They also hoped that this Messiah would deliver their nation from the bondage of the Romans by military force like King David. But they could not believe that the Messiah would be the Lord of David and the Lord of all from everlasting to everlasting.

Once Jesus Christ asked the Pharisees:

"What do you think about the Christ? Whose son is He?"

"The son of David," they replied. (They had studied prophecies from the Scriptures!)

Jesus said to them, "How is it then that David, speaking by the Spirit, calls Him 'Lord'? For he says,

"The Lord said to my Lord:

'Sit at my right hand until I put your enemies under your feet.'

If then David calls Him 'Lord' how can He be his son?"(Matthew 22:41-45)

The Pharisees could not answer this question. St. Matthew records it as follows: "No one could say a word in reply, from that day on no one dared to ask Him any more questions." (Matthew 22: 46)

The question was about the Messiah, the promised King found the Jewish Scriptures. The Pharisees knew that Jesus was quoting from Psalm 110:1, *"The Lord said to my Lord: 'Sit at my right hand until I make your enemies a footstool for your feet.*" There was no controversy among them about the interpretation of this verse. Jesus did not ask them anything outside their own book. He was asking them a simple and straight forward question which is basic truth of the Old Testament. It was not a difficult puzzle and even a child could answer this question. Then why did the expert teachers of the Law fail to answer? Even though they were scholars of the Old Testament prophecies they could not believe their Messiah would be a **Man** who would possess all the divine qualities and a **Man** who would be God Himself. For them it was blasphemy. That was the reason why they started to stone Him when He said, "**Before Abraham was born, I am!**" (John 8:58,59)

Puruṣa - The Firstborn

Now, we have to note a significant phrase about the **Man** in the **Puruṣasūkta.** In the 7th verse we read: **"Puruṣaṃ jātamagrataḥ" (The Man who is the first born.)**

In the commentary of the **Puruṣasūkta** Sayanacarya writes:

"Pūrvaṃ Puruṣaṃ jātaṃ" which means **Puruṣa was born in the beginning.** The same expression about the **Puruṣa** is found in the **Yajurveda: "Pūrvoḥ jātaḥ."**[45] **Yajurveda** continues this portion as follows:

"Before Him there was nothing."[46]

About the Lord Jesus Christ the Holy Bible says: *"He is the image of the invisible God, the firstborn over all creation. For by Him all things were created: things in heaven and on earth, visible and invisible...; all things were created by Him and for Him. He is before all things, and in Him all things hold together."* (*Colossians* 1:15-17) And again in the book of Hebrews we read the same phrase, the firstborn :**"When God brings His firstborn into this world..."** (Hebrews 1: 6)

According to the Vedas, there was nothing before **Puruṣa the firstborn.** However, the above verse in the book of Hebrews says God brought His firstborn into this world. Is God different from Puruṣa? We have seen earlier that **Prajāpati**, the supreme God, and **Puruṣa** are one and the same Person. The above quoted verse from the book of Colossians also gives us a clear answer: The Man Christ Jesus who came into this world is the image of the invisible God. Then where is the invisible God? He is in heaven and His presence is everywhere in this universe. As we read in the **Puruṣasūkta,** three quarters of God's glory is in heaven. Only one quarter of His majesty appeared here. But in Him the fullness of God dwells in bodily form even when He appeared on earth as a **Man.** Then, what does it mean when the **Puruṣasūkta** says, "only a quarter of His majesty appeared here"? The fullness of God was hidden in Christ but He voluntarily humbled and limited Himself and came down to this earth. But does this **Puruṣa** have a beginning? No, He is eternal and everlasting and He has no beginning or end. In short, we can say that in this **Man** Christ Jesus dwells the fullness of God. Here we have to note one of the definitions of **Puruṣa** in the Sanskrit language: **"Pūrṇatvāt Puruṣaḥ". (One who is perfection is the Puruṣa.)**

The Mystery is Revealed

In this light of revelation, a very difficult portion of the **Upaniṣads** becomes very clear like sunlight at noon day. Here is the verse from the **Śāntipātham** of the **Īśavāsyopaniṣad:**

"Om pūrṇamadaḥ pūrṇamidaṃ

pūrṇātpūrṇamudacyate

pūrṇasya pūrṇamādāya

pūrṇamevā- avaśiṣyate."[47]

(Om. That is full, this is full. Fullness originates from fullness. Remove fullness from fullness and fullness remains.)

Beyond any doubt we can say, this fullness (perfection) is found in God only. From this perfection, from the fullness of God (**Prajā+ pati = The Lord of all**), the perfect and sinless **Man Christ Jesus (Puruṣa)** came into this world. *("From the full, full originates.")* St.John testifies: *"We have seen His glory, the glory of the One and Only, who came from the Father, full of grace and truth."* (John 1:14) *John the Baptist also preached about His fullness: "From the fullness of His grace we have all received one blessing after another."* (John 1:16) *Fullness of God in* **Puruṣa** *on earth took nothing away from the fullness of God in heaven.* "Taking away the full from the full, the full still remains behind." In fact, God and the Puruṣa are inseparable and God is in Puruṣa and Puruṣa in God.

The incarnation of God meets its purpose through His sacrifice.

See the 16th verse of the **Puruṣasūkta:**

"Yajñena yajñamajayanta devas

tāni dharmāṇi prathamānyāsan

Teha nākaṃ mahimānaḥ+sacanta

Yatra pūrve sādhyaḥ santidevaḥ."

(The gods sacrificed Puruṣa as the sacrifice. This is the earliest established principle. Through this the sages obtain heaven.)

This is the supreme sacrifice because God Himself is the sacrificial victim and heaven is its altar. The result is the creation of the world and it is the earliest established principle. Hence this is the model of all sacrifices and the way to heaven.

Sacrifice in the Heart of God (Mānasayāgaṃ)

Sayanacarya, the ancient commentator of the **Puruṣasūkta,** wrote in Sanskrit that this sacrifice was performed in the heart of God:

("Mānasayāgaṃ niṣpāditavanta... Prajāpatiprāṇarūpa yajñena yathoktena mānasena saṃkalpena yajñaṃ...)[48]

It means this sacrifice was not literally done in heaven. But it is the blue-print of the eternal and perfect sacrifice of God which is for the salvation of mankind. N. J. Shende also points out that the sacrifice in the heart of God in heaven is "mental or symbolic one."[49]

Heavenly beings do not need a sacrifice for salvation since they are already in heaven. But the earthly man needs this perfect sacrifice for the remission of his sin which is the reason for his separation from God and heaven.

In fact, God loved man and made His eternal plan for salvation even before the creation of mankind. The Lamb that was slain from the creation of the world" is His eternal blue-print for the salvation of mankind. It stands firm in heaven. Therefore, this is the first phase of the sacrifice.

Chapter 2

THE SACRIFICE

CAME DOWN TO THE PLANET EARTH

The idea of the incarnation of God and His sacrifice was not foreign to the people of ancient India. In fact, it was very deeply rooted in their hearts. Consequently the sages expressed this concept in many ways throughout the Upaniṣads and Vedic literature.[50]

Aśvattha Tree That Came Down from Heaven

A famous verse from the **Kaṭhopaniṣad** describes the manifestation of God on earth in a beautiful and powerful image:

"Ūrdhvamūlo avāk'śākha eṣo aśvatthaḥ sanātanaḥ.

Tadeva śukraṃ tad-Braḥma tadevāmṛtamucyate.

Tasminllokāḥ śritaḥ sarve tad nātyeti kaścan etad vaitat."[51]

The translation of this portion may be quoted from the book entitled <u>The Sacred Books of the Hindus</u>:

"With roots above and the branches below, this (manifested Braḥma) is as an ancient Aśvattha tree, that indeed is the bright one that is Braḥma, that indeed is called immortal. In Him all worlds are contained, Him verily nothing goes beyond. This is that."[52]

The theme of the verse is a tree. But on close observation we find that the description is not about an ordinary tree. Look at the features of the tree. First of all, the tree is immortal. And it is bright. The word **Śukraṃ** is translated here as bright but a more appropriate meaning of the word is holy. Who is the holy and the eternal One? We have the answer in the verse itself: **"that is Brahma" which means "that is God."** Therefore, beyond any doubt, we can say that the **Aśvattha tree** is symbolically representing God Himself. Then what are the other important features of the tree? It is an inverted tree. Its roots are up in heaven and its branches are seen below on earth. All other trees grow on the earth and are grounded in the earth. They grow on the nutrients of the earth. But this divine tree is unique, since its roots are up in heaven. It grows on heavenly food. Therefore the character of the tree should be divine. The fruit of the tree appears on earth, but derives its sweetness from heaven.

Look at the other features of the tree:"**In Him all worlds are contained. (In Him all worlds are sheltered.) Beyond Him verily no one can go".** He appears on the earth to give an eternal shelter to the people of the world. This verse simply reveals the idea of incarnation. It says that the eternal and immortal **Brahma** is manifested Himself in His divine qualities on earth to save mankind. This is the pre-announced message of incarnation. It is also the way of salvation for man who has fallen away from the glory of God through sin.

We have seen the beautiful narration of the incarnation of Jesus in the first chapter of the Gospel according to John. He was from the beginning and in due time He came down to this earth. Yes, Jesus is the **Aśvattha tree** who came from heaven. Jesus said,**"I am from above."** (John 8: 23) In another place Jesus said: "I am the living bread **who came down from heaven**. And if any one eats of this bread he will live forever. This bread is my flesh which I will give for the life of the world."(John 6: 51) By this verse Jesus indicates His incarnation and His sacrificial death on the cross.

Messiah the Puruṣa- The Hope of Mankind

When we look back in history we can see that mankind was always looking forward to the Saviour. The Old Testament Scriptures plainly taught that the Messiah was going to come. Seven hundred years before Jesus, the prophet Isaiah had written about His birth as follows:

"Therefore the Lord Himself will give you a sign: The virgin will be with child and will give birth to a son, and will call him Immanuel." (Isaiah 7:14)

The Israelites were looking forward to the Messiah. Judaism as a religion is still looking forward to Him but many Jewish people have discovered the Messianic qualities of Jesus and have become followers of Christ. Simeon, a righteous and devout old man of Jerusalem, was eagerly awaiting the Messiah. "It had been revealed to him by the Holy Spirit that he would not die before he had seen the Lord's Christ." (Luke 2:26). In the temple of Jerusalem Simeon took the baby Jesus in his arms and praised God, saying: "Sovereign Lord, as you have promised, now dismiss your servant in peace. *For My eyes have seen your salvation, which you have prepared in the sight of all people, a light for revelation to the Gentiles and for glory to your people Israel."* (Luke 2: 28-32)

The people of the East were also awaiting the coming of the Saviour and they called Him the **Niṣkalanka Puruṣa** which means the **sinless Man.** That was the reason the birth of Christ was announced to the sages of the East through His star. We read about this in the second chapter of the Gospel of Matthew.

The Cut-tree and the Sacrificial Puruṣa

The concept of the **Aśvattha tree** and the **Puruṣa-Prajāpati** is one and the same, and it reveals the same idea of incarnation as the way of salvation for mankind. Another name of the **Aśvattha tree** is **Vanaspati** which literally means **the Lord of the trees.**

In the **Bṛhadāraṇyaka Upaniṣad** we read:

"Yatha vṛkṣo vanaspati-

stathaiva Puruṣo amṛṣa."[53]

(As Vanaspati is to the trees so is Puruṣa. This is true. - As **Vanaspati** is superior to every tree so **Puruṣa** is superior to everybody in the world -.)

The next hymn in the Upaniṣad says, **"As the sap oozes from the cut tree so blood is being shed from the bruised Man."**

"Tvaca evasya rudhiraṃ

Prasyandi tvaca utpataḥ

Tasmāttadātṛuṇṇāt praiti

Raso vṛkṣadi vāhatāt."[54]

(Blood is dripping from the **Puruṣa**'s skin. Sap is coming out from the tree. So just as sap comes from the cut tree, blood comes from the bruised Man.)

When we compare this with the sacrifice of **Puruṣa-Prajāpati** from the **Ṛg Vedic Puruṣasūkta** we can easily see the significance of the above verses in relation to the **Aśvattha** tree or **Vanaspati. The tree came down to earth to give mankind eternal shelter through its sacrifice.** Therefore, the **cut tree** is very significant in this context. Blood is coming from the bruised **Man.** Sap is coming from the **cut tree.** Surely in this context such vivid imagery can point only to the eternal sacrifice of God. The tree that came down from heaven was manifested to the people and gave them an everlasting shelter. Since the cut-tree was compared with the **Sacrificial Puruṣa**, we can say that the sacrifice also came down just as the tree came down to earth from heaven. However, we are going to see this in the next chapter as it is the second stage of sacrifice.

"Messiah Will Be Cut Off" - The Prophecy of Daniel

"Messiah , the Anointed One, will be cut off." Thus, about six hundred B.C., Daniel the prophet had predicted the sacrificial death of Jesus Christ using the same terminology, **'cut off'**. He even prophesied the exact time of the event: **". . . After sixty-two 'sevens,' the Anointed One will be cut off."**(Daniel 9: 26) The prophet Isaiah also used the same term for the sacrifice of Jesus: **"He was cut off from the land of living."** (Isaiah 53:8)

By transferring the concept of the sacrifice of the **Puruṣa-Prajāpati**, God was revealing His eternal plan of salvation through the crucifixion of the Lord Jesus Christ, even before His incarnation. *"God who at sundry times and in divers manners spoke in times past to the fathers by the prophets, last of all in these days has spoken to us by His Son, whom He appointed heir of all things, by whom also He made the world."* (Hebrews 1:1,2) Quoting this famous verse from the Bible Raimundo Panikkar, Professor at Harvard University and the University of California, writes in his book, The Unknown Christ of Hinduism: "From this we may surmise that the Son has inspired not only the prophets of Israel but also the sages of Hinduism and that He has been present in all the endeavors of man, for we are certain that 'upholding all things by the word of His power'(Hebrews 1: 3) He has never forsaken His world."[55] Professor Panikkar wants to see Christ in Hinduism but as the title of his book suggests, Christ, the **Puruṣa,** is still unknown to Hinduism even though the **Upaniṣads** command us to know Him. The two religions of the world, Christianity and Hinduism of this day, may not agree with Mr. Panikkar regarding the revelation and the spirit of Christ in Hinduism. But we do accept his point that in Christ we are not in a position of confrontation but are standing on common ground - **a meeting place to rest.** In Him we have no division. In fact, the unity of mankind is totally dependent upon Him, the **Puruṣa-Prajāpati, the Man Christ Jesus.** Paul writes to the believers in Ephesus reminding them of their previous state of diversity and present unity in Christ: *"For He Himself is our peace, who has made the two one and has destroyed the barrier, the dividing wall of hostility. . ."* (Ephesians 2:14)

Chapter 3

SACRIFICE - SHADOW AND SUBSTANCE

The Origin of Animal-Sacrifice

Before we get into the main theme of this chapter regarding the evolution of sacrifice we have to discuss the origin of this ritual on earth. How did our fore-fathers get the idea of sacrifice for salvation. The **Ṛg Veda** says that they discovered what had been out of their reach: the supreme abode of the sacrifice, which is invisible.[56] The Veda continues this in the very next verse: "Meditating in their heart they discovered the sacrifice that has descended, the first pathway to God." In other words, we can say that God revealed to them the idea of sacrifice when they eagerly sought for the way to attain immortality. With the support of many verses from the Vedas, H. Aguilar writes: "The earthly sacrifice is the continuation of the celestial sacrifice."[57]

From the Man Sacrifice (**Puruṣa medha**) in the **Ṛg Vedic Puruṣasūkta,** we are able to see that the Man Sacrifice was performed in heaven. We have already seen in the last chapter that this sacrifice originated in the heart of God and later on He revealed it to mankind. The sacrifice came down from heaven. We can say that it was the second stage of the sacrifice. God spoke to Moses: "Speak to the sons of Israel, saying, If a person sins. . .,if the anointed priest sins so as to bring guilt on the people, then let him offer to the Lord a bull without defect as a sin offering for the sin he has committed."(Leviticus 4:3 NASB) However, before Moses there had been sacrifices as early as the time of Adam. Abel, son of Adam, offered to God a better sacrifice than his brother Cain. " And the Lord had regard for Abel and his offering." (Genesis 4:4)

The First Animal Sacrifice

The first animal sacrifice was performed in the garden of Eden. God created the first man and woman and He gave them the beautiful garden of Eden. However, they disobeyed God and sinned. From that time on they were afraid and ashamed. They knew that they were naked; they could not stand before God. When God called them they hid themselves from the presence of the Lord. God called to the man and asked him:

"Where are you?"

And he said,

"I heard the sound of Thee in the garden, and I was afraid because I was naked; so I hid myself." (Genesis 3:10)

Thus, the original relationship between God and man was broken. Man was unable to stand before God. He could not call upon Him. But the Lord God had compassion on them, the man and the woman, and He Himself sought for them. God wanted to redeem them because they were His creation. He loved them and cursed Satan who was the root cause of sin and put an everlasting enmity between Satan and mankind for the protection of His creation. Thus He said to the devil:

"And I will put enmity between you and the woman, and between your offspring and hers; *He (woman's offspring) will crush your head, and you will strike His heel."* (Genesis 3:15)

Here, in the Garden of Eden, God revealed the plan of redemption of mankind and the ultimate destruction of the Satanic kingdom. In a prophetic manner, He revealed the plan of salvation through the Lord Jesus Christ who was the offspring of the virgin Mary, the woman, and not the son of a human father. Then, in the Garden, "the Lord God made garments of **skin** for Adam and his wife, and clothed them." (Genesis 3:21) An innocent animal was killed for the sake of the man and the woman. By clothing them in animal-skin, God showed that they were forgiven. At the same time, the sacrificial animal bore the curse of sin, that is, "the wages of sin is death." (Rom.6: 23) When we study the history of man we see that people of all parts of the world and of all ages have the conception of sacrifice for the remission of sin.

Sacrifice - Shadow and Substance

As we have seen above, all the sacrifices ordained by God are symbolic representations of the sacrifice of **Prajāpati**. The mere sacrifice of animals was not sufficient in itself either to please God or to atone for sin. God was pleased only because all these sacrifices represented the sacrifice of Prajāpati, the Supreme God. By offering an animal, the sacrificers were actually symbolizing the sacrifice of the eternal God which is intended for the forgiveness of sin. The Holy Spirit reveals this through the words of David in the Book of Psalms: "Sacrifice and meal offering Thou hast not desired; . . . Burnt offering and sin offering Thou hast not required." (Psalms 40:6)

The Holy Spirit explains this fact more clearly in the **New Testament** as follows:

"For it is impossible for the blood of bulls and goats to take away sins. Therefore, when He comes to the world, He says, 'sacrifice and offering Thou hast not desired, but a body Thou hast prepared for Me; in whole burnt offerings and sacrifices for sin Thou hast taken no pleasure.' Then I said, 'Behold I have come (In the scroll of the book it is written of Me) to do Thy will, O God.' " (Hebrews 10: 4-7) The will of God was to make a perfect sacrifice through the offering of God Himself. For that purpose He needed a body in order to offer this sacrifice on the earth. In the **Bṛhadāraṇyaka Upaniṣad** we read that Prajāpati, the Supreme God, wished for a body to be offered.[58] This is fulfilled in the incarnation of Jesus. God became flesh and dwelt among us. The Son of God became the Son of Man; **Prajāpati** became **Puruṣa** (Man). And He was delighted to fulfill the will of the Father Almighty. The Scripture says: "By this will we have been sanctified through the offering through the body of Jesus Christ once for all."(Hebrews 10:10 NASB) In another place we read: "When Christ came as high priest of good things that are already here, he went through the greater and more perfect tabernacle that is not man-made, that is to say, not a part of this creation. He did not enter by means of the blood of goats and calves; but He entered the Most Holy Place once for all by His own blood, having obtained eternal redemption. The blood of goats and bulls and the ashes of a heifer sprinkled on those who are ceremonially unclean sanctify them so that they are outwardly clean. How much more, then, will the blood of Christ, who through the eternal Spirit offered Himself unblemished to God, cleanse our consciences from acts that lead to death, so that we may serve the living God."(Hebrews 9:11-14.) "He, having offered one sacrifice for sins for all time, sat down at the right hand of God."(Hebrews 10:12.NASB)

By that perfect sacrifice He has fulfilled all other old sacrifices. The Holy Bible says: "By one sacrifice he has made perfect forever those who are being made holy." (Hebrews 10:14) To them God says: "Their sins and lawless acts I will remember no more." (Hebrews 10:17) By that perfect sacrifice He has completed the redemptive work and therefore it is written in this context as follows: "And where these have been forgiven, there is no longer any sacrifice for sin." (v.18) Once the Supreme Sacrifice has been made, there is no further need for animal-sacrifices.

The Old Testament and Sacrifices

According to the Old Testament Scriptures the way of redemption is through sacrifice. All the references to sacrifice are fulfilled in the crucifixion of the Lord Jesus Christ. There are many prophecies about the sacrifice of Jesus in the Old Testament, the religious text of the Israelites, written before Christ. I am only touching the subject to point out the clarity of such prophecies. Jesus Christ Himself taught His disciples that the meaning of His sacrificial death was explained in the Scriptures. He says, "**The Son of Man will go just as it is written about Him.**"(Matthew 26: 24) Jesus said to the Jews who refused to believe Him, "You diligently study the Scriptures because you think that by them you possess eternal life. **These are Scriptures that testify about Me, . . .**"(John 5: 39) To them He continued, "If you believed Moses, you would believe Me, **for he wrote about Me**." (v.46) Even His own disciples were slow of heart to believe that Christ had to go through sufferings and sacrifice. After the resurrection, Jesus Christ appeared to the disciples and said to them, "How foolish you are, and how slow of heart to believe all that **the prophets have spoken!** Did not the Christ have to suffer these things and then enter His glory?" (Luke 24:25,26) St. Luke continued in the next verse: "And beginning with Moses and all the Prophets, He explained to them what was said in all the Scriptures concerning Himself." (v.27) Again Jesus said to them, *"This is what I have told you while I was still with you: Everything must be fulfilled that is written about Me in the Law of Moses, the Prophets and the Psalms."* (v.44) Jesus Himself pointed out that His coming was foretold in the Old Testament.

Isaiah, one of the prophets, portrayed the suffering Saviour over 700 years before the Saviour's birth. His narration is so vivid and in such detail, "that one would almost think of Isaiah as standing at the foot of the cross."[59] Isaiah called this Man a suffering Servant. "He was despised and rejected by men, a Man of sorrows, and familiar with suffering." (Isaiah 53:3) Jesus was rejected by His own and this is also one of the important characteristics of the Prajāpati-Sacrifice according to the Vedas which we will see later.[60] The substitutionary aspect of the atonement was also predicted by Isaiah as follows:

"But He was pierced for our transgressions, He was crushed for our iniquities; the punishment that brought us peace was upon Him, and by His wounds we are healed." (Isaiah 53:5)

Christ Jesus came into the world to save sinners and He died for our sins. Isaiah continued his description about the sacrifice of the suffering Servant as follows:

"He was oppressed and afflicted, yet He did not open His mouth; He was led like a lamb to the slaughter, and as a sheep before her shearers is silent, so He did not open His mouth... He was cut off from the land of the living; for the transgression of my people He was stricken . . . though He had done no violence, nor was any deceit in his mouth." (verses 7-9).

This sacrifice of the suffering Servant was God's plan of salvation to all the world. Isaiah makes it clear in the next verse:

" Yet it was the LORD'S will to crush Him and cause Him to suffer, and . . . the LORD makes His life a guilt offering, . . (v.10)

The Sacrifice and gods

According to the Vedas Prajāpati offered Himself for gods. From the **Tāndymahābrāhmaṇa** we have seen this earlier.[61] In the **Puruṣasūkta** gods offered Puruṣa-Prajāpati in the sacrifice.[62] Who are these gods? By His sacrifice Christ made atonement for human beings, not for gods. Let us examine who these gods are in the light of the Scriptures. In the Gospel of John, we read that men were called gods. When Christ said that He was the Son of God, the Jews interpreted His statement as blasphemy. In this context Jesus answered them as follows:

"Is it not written in your Law, 'I have said you are gods?' If he called them 'gods,'to whom the word of God came - and the Scripture cannot be broken - what about the one whom the Father set apart as His very own and sent into the world?" (John 10: 34,35) The Holy Bible calls them'gods' to whom the word of God came. And the Lord Jesus Christ, the Son of God, attested to the truth of the statement. From the verse it is clear that those gods are human beings.

The Vedas use the term, **'devas'** for gods. According to Vedic literature, these gods are born of **ṛta** (sacrifice). We have numerous references for this, such as -"**Ṛtajāta**","**Ṛtaja**", "**Ṛtaprajāta**", etc. which are all significant expressions for gods. All these words indicate one who is born of **ṛta** (sacrifice). In what sense can someone be born of sacrifice? Thus the Lord says in the book of Psalms: "Gather to Me My consecrated ones, who made a covenant with Me with sacrifice." (Psalm 50:5) Now it is quite clear that the gods are the people who are born again of the sacrifice of Prajāpati. Jesus says: "Truly, truly, I say to you, unless one is born again, he cannot see the kingdom of God." (John 3: 3) In other words, we can say that those who believe in the sacrifice of Jesus Christ as atonement for their sins would be called the sons of God. The Bible says: "Yet to all who received Him, to those who believed in His name, He gave the right to become children of God."(John 1:12). To those who believe in Him, the Holy Spirit would say: "See how great a love the Father has bestowed upon us, that we should be called children of God; and such we are."(1.John 3:1) Only those who believe that Christ made Himself a sacrifice for their sins will benefit from that atonement, and will be called the sons of God. So figuratively, the children of God can be called gods. Here, the statement of the Vedas, that Prajāpati offered Himself for the gods, is fulfilled through the results of Christ's crucifixion. In the Old Testament, the prophet Isaiah also concluded his prophetical description about the crucifixion almost the same way, highlighting the result of the sacrifice. The suffering servant, the Man of sorrows (the sacrificial victim) will see His children and be satisfied.

The verse says,
"...and though the LORD makes His life a guilt offering, He will see His offspring and prolong His days, and the will of the LORD will prosper in His hand. After the suffering of His soul, He will see the light of life and be satisfied; by His knowledge my righteous servant will justify many, and He will bear their iniquities." (Isaiah 53: 10,11)

Yes,"He Himself is the propitiation for our sins and not for ours only, but also those of the whole world." (1.John.2:2)

Chapter 4

JESUS - THE SACRIFICIAL LAMB

Behold the Lamb!

"Behold the Lamb of God who takes away the sin of the world!" (John 1: 29) Just before Jesus started His public ministry, John the Baptist introduced Jesus to the world as the sacrificial lamb of God.

Why did John called Him 'Lamb'? Jesus was not an animal but a man. Then what is the significance of calling Him 'Lamb'? The lamb was the most prominent sacrificial animal in the Old Testament and in Vedic literature for the forgiveness of sin.[63] God commanded the Jews to sacrifice a lamb on the Passover. The conception of the Passover lamb was deep-rooted in the hearts of Israelites. On every Passover night, year by year, the Jewish people slaughtered the Passover lamb foreshadowing God's perfect sacrifice; the only sacrifice able to propitiate the sins of the people and establish a permanent celebration of victory and freedom. Therefore, when the real Passover Lamb came in this world to fulfill the significance of all sacrifices, John the Baptist cried out in the Spirit of the Lord: "Behold the Lamb of God who takes away the sin of the world."

After Jesus' crucifixion and the resurrection St.Paul writes, *"For Christ, our Passover lamb, has been sacrificed."* (1. Cor. 5: 7) Pointing out the result of the sacrifice St. Peter writes, "For you know that it was not with perishable things such as silver or gold that you were redeemed from the empty way of life. . .but with the precious blood of Christ, a lamb without blemish or defect." (1. Peter 1: 18,19) In the book of Revelation we can see this Lamb who is worthy to be worshipped. In a loud voice the heavenly creatures and the twenty four elders of heaven sang before this Lamb who had given Himself in sacrifice:

"Worthy is the Lamb, who was slain, to receive power and wealth and wisdom and strength and honour and glory and praise!" (Revelation 5:12)

When we study Vedic literature we see that the lamb was the common animal for sacrifices. The ordinance of sacrifices can be seen in the **Brāḥmaṇas Texts** where the lamb is also featured prominently.[64]

JESUS EXPLAINS THE MEANING OF SACRIFICE

The central point of the teaching of the Lord Jesus Christ is His own sacrifice. From the beginning of His public ministry Jesus began to teach them about His own sacrificial death. St. Matthew writes: "Jesus began to explain to His disciples that He must go to Jerusalem and suffer many things at the hands of the elders, the chief priests and teachers of the law, and that He must be killed and on the third day be raised to life." (Matthew 16:21) At another place, He said to them, "The Son of Man did not come to be served but to serve and to give **His life as a ransom for many**." (Matthew 20: 28) When Jesus taught Nicodemus, a Jewish councillor, about eternal life He said, "Just as Moses lifted up the snake in the desert, so **the Son of Man must be lifted up,** that everyone who believes in Him may have eternal life." (John 3:14) By this **the Son of Man (Puruṣa)** meant His own sacrificial death. On another occasion, Jesus said, "But I, when I am lifted up from the earth, will draw all men to myself".(John 12: 32) St. John made it clear what He meant in the next verse: "He said this to show the kind of death He was going to die." (verse 33) In order to explain the meaning of His sacrifice, Jesus talked to them figuratively: "I am the living bread. . .If anyone eats of this bread, he will live forever. This bread is **my flesh**, which I will give for the life of the world." (John 6: 51) Again He said: "I am the good shepherd. The good shepherd lays down his life for the sheep. ..Greater love has no one than this, that he lay down his life for his friends." (John 10:11 & 15:13) Jesus explained the concept of sacrifice in many ways. The sacrifice of Christ involves love, self-denial, covenant, blood-shed and burning. Surely, it is the greatest manifestation of love that the world has ever seen.

Before deciding to go to Jerusalem to drink the bitter cup

Jesus spoke these words to His disciples:

"We are going up to Jerusalem, and everything that is written by the prophets about the Son of Man will be fulfilled. He will be handed over to the Gentiles. They will mock Him, insult Him, spit on Him, flog Him and kill Him. On the third day He will rise again." (Luke18: 31-33)

The Significance of Hosanna

The next day people heard that Jesus was on the wayto Jerusalem. He rode on a donkey accompanied by His disciples. (People thought that the Kingdom of God was going to appear at once. [Luke 19: 11]) Taking palm branches in their hands they glorified Jesus shouting, "Hosanna! Blessed is He who comes in the name of the Lord!" (John 12:13) They were praising Jesus by singing and shouting **Hosanna,** a Hebrew expression meaning 'save' which became an exclamation of praise. How appropriate this welcome song of Hosanna is within the context of the Saviour of the world appearing on the scene to offer Himself in God's program of redemptive activity! "To save people from their sins" is His mission and because of this mission He was given the name Jesus. (Matthew 1:21) Even though the people did not understand fully what was going to happen, by the help of the Holy Spirit they were rightly singing the Hosanna song and acknowledging the mission of the Lord Jesus Christ. When they sang Hosanna they were glorifying Him by giving proper recognition to His mission of salvation for all mankind. Everything happened according to the sacred prophetic writings about Him. St. John quotes from Zechariah 9: 9 in this context: "Do not be afraid, O Daughter of Zion; see, your king is coming seated on a donkey's colt." At this point John writes as follows: "At first His disciples did not understand all this. Only after Jesus was glorified did they realize that these things had been written about Him and that they had done these things to Him." (John 12:16)

Jesus Predicts the Exact Time of His Sacrifice

As the time for His sacrificial death approached, Jesus said, "The hour has come for the Son of Man to be glorified. I tell you the truth, unless a kernel of wheat falls to the ground and dies, it remains only a single seed. But if it dies it produces many seeds." (John 12: 23, 24) On their way up to Jerusalem, " Jesus took the Twelve aside and told them again what was going to happen to Him." (Mark 10: 33-34)

Two days before the Passover feast Jesus said,

"As you know, the Passover is two days away - and the Son of Man will be handed over to be crucified" (Matthew 26:2)

Just before the Passover Feast, Jesus washed the feet of His disciples. Concerning this, St. John writes significantly: "He knew that the time had come for Him to leave this world and go to the Father." (John 13:1) Jesus predicted His betrayal by His own disciple. He said, "I tell you the truth, one of you is going to betray Me." (John 13:21) He said, "I am telling you now before it happens so that when it does happen you will believe that I am He." (John 13:19) The expression, **'I am He'** is very significant. He was saying that they would understand and believe that Jesus was the **Man (the Puruṣa)** about whom the Sacred books have spoken. He was the **'Man of sorrows'** who was despised and rejected by men.

Jesus continued to say, "My children, I will be with you only a little longer. . ." (John 13: 33) "Do not let your hearts be troubled. . . .I am going to prepare a place for you. And if I go and prepare a place for you, I will come back and take you to be with Me that you also may be where I am." (John 14:1-3)

After Jesus gave them the words of comfort and counseling He started to pray:

"Father, the time has come. Glorify your Son, that your Son may glorify you. For you granted Him authority over all people that He might give eternal life to all those you have given Him. Now this is eternal life: that they may KNOW You the only true God,and Jesus Christ, whom You have sent." (John 17:1-3)

Remember the verse we have quoted earlier from the **Kaṭhopaniṣad:**

"One who KNOWS Him (the Puruṣa, the Man) becomes free and attains immortality." [65]

Even though the disciples were very slow to accept His

sacrificial death, Jesus taught them the vicarious nature of His sacrifice very clearly.

The Last Supper

On the night before His crucifixion, at the time of His last supper, Jesus took bread, gave thanks and broke it, and gave it to His disciples, saying, **"Take and eat; this is My body."** Then He took the cup and said, "Drink from it, all of you. This is My blood of the covenant, which is poured out for many for the forgiveness of sins." (Matthew 26:26,27). It was the most important Passover night in Jewish history as well as in the history of the whole world. On that night shadow and substance came together. When the Passover lamb was being sacrificed in the temple, the heavenly Father set apart His own precious Son, the Lamb of God, in order that He might become a sacrifice for the whole world.

The Last Preparation in the Garden of Gethsemane

After the supper, He stayed awake throughout the night at the garden of Gethsemane. He was praying, overwhelmed with sorrow. Three disciples were with Him. To them He said:

"My soul is overwhelmed with sorrow to the point of death. Stay here and keep watch with Me." (Matthew 26:38)

"Going a little further, He fell with His face to the ground and prayed,

'My Father, if it is possible, may this cup be taken from Me. Yet not as I will, but as you will." (Matthew 26:39)

When Jesus returned from prayer the disciples were sleeping. Jesus said to them,

"Are you still sleeping and resting? Look, the hour is near, and the Son of Man is betrayed into the hands of sinners. Rise, let us go! Here comes My betrayer!" (verse 45)

He Gave Himself

Judas, one of the twelve disciples, entered the scene with a large crowd armed with swords and clubs. Judas kissed Jesus. Jesus responded:

"Friend, do what you came for." St. John records this as

follows: "Jesus knowing all that was going to happen to Him, went out and asked them,

'Who is it you want?'"

'Jesus of Nazareth,' they replied.

'I am He,' Jesus said...When Jesus said, 'I am He' they drew back and fell to the ground.

Again He asked them,

'Who is it you want?'

And they said,

'Jesus of Nazareth.'

'I told you that I am He' Jesus answered." (John 18:4-8)

He gave Himself to them to be sacrificed. When He said, "I am He," He was identifying Himself as the sacrificial Lamb of God. He was telling all the world that He was the real and perfect sacrifice of **Puruṣa-Prajāpati** which is the culmination of God's plan for the salvation of mankind.

Jesus was taken to Annas, who was the father-in-law of Caiaphas, the high priest that year. Then He was brought to Caiaphas. Even though Caiaphas was spiritually blind he was holding a most holy office ordained by God. As Jesus said, "Pharisees sit in Moses' seat." (Matthew 23: 2) As God gave Moses a part in prophesying about God's program of the redemptive sacrifice of **the Puruṣa-Prajāpati- the Lord Jesus Christ**, God also gave Caiaphas, the high priest of the year, a role in the redemptive sacrifice of God. He was the one who had convinced the Jews that it would be good if one man died for the people. St. John narrated this as follows: "Then one of them, named Caiaphas, who was high priest that year, spoke up, 'You know nothing at all! You do not realize that it is better for you **that one man (Puruṣa)** *die for the people than that the whole nation perish.''*...(John 11:50) St. John continues to write: *"He did not say this on his own, but as high priest that year he prophesied that Jesus would die for the Jewish nation, and not only for that nation but also for the scattered children of God, to bring them together and make them one."* (verse 51) Priests were supposed to perform the sacrifice. Now most willingly Jesus gave Himself to the priests. As Jesus said, "The time has come." He received the cross most willingly. Carrying His own cross, He went out to the mount of Golgotha. There He was crucified. Thus the love of God reached its climax through His offering. On the cross Jesus said meaningfully, *"It is finished."* (John 19:30)

The Third Stage - The Climax of the Sacrifice

The actual sacrifice is performed at this stage. "The Lamb was slain from the creation of the world" is the first stage. In the second stage it appears on the earth and is continued through the animal-sacrifices until Christ's eternal sacrifice is performed. Thus all other sacrifices- the symbols of Christ's sacrifice - are fulfilled and totally terminated by the powerful word of Jesus on the cross, **"It is finished."** When Jesus gave up His spirit the curtain of the temple was torn in two **from top to bottom** . It was God's hand that came down from heaven to tear the temple curtain since it was torn from top to bottom. When God did it, He did it meaningfully. It proclaims two things:

(1) God put an end to the temple sacrifices.

(2) God opened for us through the curtain a new and living way to the presence of God. Through the death of Jesus the curtain between man and God is eternally removed. Therefore we can go into the presence of the Lord anytime with a sincere heart in full assurance of faith. (Hebrews 10:20-21)

When we study the Gospels we can easily see that the Lord Jesus was looking forward to His own sacrifice. He Himself prepared to be sacrificed and He was preparing His own disciples to share the Cross. He explained and revealed to His children the mystery of sacrifice.

As long as one does not understand the mystery of sacrifice, it is a foolish act of bloodshed. That is the reason why even some great scholars consider the death of the Lord Jesus to be a tragedy. Swami Ranganathananda writes in his book, The Christ We Adore, as follows: "To us in India, however, the end (the end of Jesus) is just a tragedy, bereft of any spiritual beauty".[66] But at the same time Swami says that Christ is worthy to be worshipped and he seems to feel deeply a personal sadness for the crucifixion. Sacrifice is foolishness if one does not find the real substance of the shadow. But God has given us the sacrifice (**Yajña**) of His Son as the way of salvation. Whenever the true sages of the ancients performed sacrifices, they looked forward to the cross of Jesus and identified with the cross for their salvation. The Holy Bible says: *"The message of the cross is foolishness to those who are perishing, but to us who are being saved it is the power of God."* (1.Cor.1:18)

PART II

THE TEN CHARACTERISTICS AND THE RESULTS OF THE PRAJĀPATI-SACRIFICE FULFILLED IN JESUS' CRUCIFIXION AND RESURRECTION

PART II

"Asatomā satgamaya - From the unreal lead me to truth." The sages searched for truth with great sincerity and humility by confessing their inability to attain the perfect truth. In answer to their prayer God showed us the path of the perfect sacrifice of Prajāpati. The most important benefit of this sacrifice is suggested in the **Kaṭhopaniṣad** in the verse starting: *"Ṛitam pibantau sukṛtasya loke. . ."*[67] Here the sacrificers are described as drinkers of the truth. They are enjoying the truth as the result of good works. From the next half of the verse we can understand that good works are to follow the path of sacrifice.

Truth becomes clear as noon day when we consider the features of the sacrifice. Those special features and their fulfillments make this Prajāpati-sacrifice unique and supreme.

Vedic Literature shows us at least ten important features of the Prajāpati-Sacrifice which are completely fulfilled in Jesus' crucifixion and resurrection. The outstanding results of the Vedic sacrifices are also present in the results of Christ's crucifixion. The fruit of a sacrifice can be seen in its believers. According to Vedic thought, the sacrificer identifies with the victim of the sacrifice. When we come to the sacrifice of the crucifixion we can also see that the believer identifies with the cross. This is the final stage of the sacrifice, in which the believer achieves total identification. It is only at this stage that the fruits of the sacrifice are bestowed upon the believer. The fourth stage of sacrifice is the *'living sacrifice'*.

Chapter 5

CHARACTERISTIC # 1

THE NIṢKALANKA PURUṢA

(THE SINLESS MAN)

Sacrificial Man Should be Blameless

Man on earth is always conscious of his sinful nature. He wants to be free from blame. Yet he turns to sin naturally. He wants to be free from slavery to his sinful nature. That was the reason why the sages looked forward to the **Niṣkalanka Puruṣa,** the Sinless Man. They knew about God's sinless nature but they could not identify with God because God is a God who abides in the glorious light beyond the reach of man on earth. Therefore they were looking for a Perfect Man having all the divine qualities of God for a perfect example and a perfect model to follow.

The Sinless Man in the Vedas and in the Holy Bible

The sacrificial Man in the **Puruṣasūkta** should be blameless. This is the most important characteristic of the **Puruṣa Prajāpati**'s sacrifice. Since the sacrifice originated in the heart of God in heaven it has to be perfect and its victim should be sinless.

These features can be seen in the Man-Sacrifice of the **Puruṣasūkta** . The **Chāndogya Upaniṣad,** one of the Upaniṣads written before the Christian era, also praises the sinless character of **Puruṣa** as follows:

"This Man is above all sin and one who worships Him and follows Him also raises himself above sin."[68]

We can see the significance of the word **'Puruṣa'** in the **Bṛhadāraṇyaka Upaniṣad** in connection with His sinlessness. The text defined the name **Puruṣa** as follows:

" Sa yat pūrvo asmāt sarvasmāt sarvān pāpmana auṣat tasmāt Puruṣaḥ.

(He who burned out all sins before all - everyone - is Puruṣa.)[69]

According to this, the derivation of the word **'Puruṣa'** is from **'pūrvaṃ'** (before or being in front of) and **'oṣah'** (burning). The Man burns out sin. The verb 'burn' is commonly used in connection with fire. Fire burns out any impurities. At the same time fire remains pure. Gold and silver go through fire for purification. In the same manner there is no impurity in **Puruṣa** and He burns out all other impurities. In short we can say that the concept of the **Puruṣa** is holy from the beginning. The sacrificial Lamb of God in heaven, the Lamb who was slain before the foundation of the world, is also unique in His character of holiness and sinlessness.

Blameless Victims in the Old Testament Sacrifices

When the sacrifice came down from heaven to earth at the second stage there were strict ordinances requiring that the sacrificial animal be blameless. "The animals you choose must be year old males without defect. . ." (Exodus 12: 5) "Do not bring anything with a defect, because it will not be accepted on your behalf." (Leviticus 22:20) Thus the Holy Bible always demanded blameless sacrifices. We have similar portions in Vedic writings like **Kātyāyana Śrautasūtraṃ.** The text demands to purify the sacrificial animal through water and fire.[70]

Who Is Blameless in the World?

However, in the strict sense, a human being is unable to produce a sinless victim for the sacrifice. Where can we find a blameless creature in this world? All men, women, animals, and all living beings in this world are under the curse of sin. According to the Scriptures, everything in the world is cursed because of man's sin. (Genesis 3:14-19) All are imperfect. In God's sight everybody is a sinner. As it is written,

"There is no one righteous, not even one; there is no one who understands, no one who seeks God. All have turned away, they have together become worthless; there is no one who does good, not even one." (Romans 3:10-12)

No one is able to stand before God and open his mouth since "every mouth may be closed and all the world become accountable to God." (Romans 3:19) As Isaiah writes: "For all of us have become like one who is unclean, and all our righteous deeds are like a filthy garment." (Isaiah 64:6) The Apostle John heard a challenging proclamation of the angel in the book of Revelation: "Who is worthy to open the book and break its seals?" (Revelation 5:2) That book is the book of redemption. St. John continues to write: "And no one in heaven, or on the earth, or under the earth, was able to open the book, or to look into it." (Revelation 5:3) Therefore, John wept greatly. No one was found worthy to open the book and to perform the perfect sacrifice and redeem fallen man. Then, John heard a sound:"Stop weeping; behold, the Lion that is from the tribe of Judah, and the root of David, (Jesus) has overcome so as to open the book and its seven seals." (verse 5. NASB). In the very next verse he saw the vision of the perfect sacrifice. He writes:

"I saw between the throne (with the four living creatures) and the elders a Lamb standing as if slain,...." (verse 6.)

Worthy is the Lamb because He was slain as the perfect sacrifice. He is the sinless Lamb of God who takes away the sin of the world.

The Sinless Life of Jesus Christ

When we carefully examine the life of Jesus Christ we can clearly see that "**in Him there was no sin.**" (1.John 3:5) This is an important statement. Nobody can make this claim other than Jesus. The Lord Jesus Christ performed His ministry publicly in view of His disciples and His enemies. Very often He was accompanied by a great multitude.

Jesus was an open book to everybody. Every single step of Jesus was closely watched, checked, analyzed and criticized by His enemies. The Scribes and Pharisees always tried to find fault with

Him. Several times they questioned Him "in order that they might accuse Him" (Matthew 12:10). When Jesus healed the paralytic saying, "**Son,your sins are forgiven,**" the Scribes, the teachers of the Law, murmured: "This fellow is blaspheming!" Knowing their thoughts, Jesus said, "Why do you entertain evil thoughts in your hearts? Which is easier to say, 'Your sins are forgiven' or to say, 'Get up and walk'? But so that you may know that the Son of Man has authority on earth to forgive sins. . ." The paralytic took his own bed and went home. The crowd was filled with awe; and they praised God while the accusers silently hid themselves. (Matthew 9:1-8)

When the Lord Jesus drove devils out from the demon-possessed people, His accusers said, "It is only by Beelzebub, the prince of demons, that this fellow drives out demons." Hearing this Jesus said to them, "Every kingdom divided against itself will not stand. If Satan drives out Satan he is divided against himself. How then can his kingdom stand?. . . But if I drive out demons by the Spirit of God, then the kingdom of God has come upon you. . ." (Matthew 12:24-28).

Jesus continued His healing ministry even on the Sabbath days. Seeing this they said, "This man is not from God, for He does not keep the Sabbath." But the people who experienced His healing powers asked them, "How can a sinner do such miraculous signs?" (John 9:16) The blind received sight, the lame walked, the lepers were cleansed, the deaf heard and the dead were raised to life; they could not remain silent. Defending the accusation about keeping the Sabbath Jesus said, "If any of you has a sheep and it falls into a pit on the Sabbath, will you not take hold of it and lift it out? How much more valuable is a man than a sheep! Therefore it is lawful to do good on the Sabbath." (Matthew 12:11) On another occasion Jesus challenged them saying, *"Can any of you prove Me guilty of sin?"* (John 8:46) Yes, He was the **Niṣkalanka Puruṣa** who was set apart for the sacrifice of Prajā-pati. As the sages say, He was the eternal and sinless **Aśvattha tree** that came down from heaven. Here is the **Man!** "Have thou nothing to do with that **JUST MAN.**" - That was the warning to Pilate, the Roman judge, from his wife. (Matthew 27:19.KJV) Yes He was the **JUST MAN.** In the court of the Romans, after Jesus was tried by Pilate He declared to the Jews:

"Behold, having examined Him before you, I have found no guilt in this Man (Purusa) regarding the charges which you make against Him. No, nor has Herod, for he sent Him back to us." (Luke 23:14,15 NASB)

He affirmed three times that he could not find any guilt in Him and finally he washed his hands in front of the crowd saying, "I am innocent of this **Man's** blood." (John 18:38; 19:4-6; Matthew 27:24)

The Trial of Jesus

Pilate was the authorised person to declare the sinlessness of the **Man.** He was holding a very important position. He was appointed Procurator of Judea by the Roman Emperor. J. C. McRuer writes in his book, "In the name of the Emperor, Pilate exercised executive, military and judicial power. From his decisions there was no appeal except Caesar."[71] That is why Pilate said to Jesus: "Don't you realize I have power either to free you or to crucify You?" Jesus answered, "You would have no power over Me if it were not given to you from above." (John 19:10,11) When Pilate said that he could not find any basis for a charge against Him, he was inadvertently attesting to His spotlessness and fitness to be the sacrificial lamb. As the sinless lamb He was worthy to be the victim for the **Prajāpati-Sacrifice** intended for the remission of sin and attaining immortality. As Caiaphas, the high priest of the year, unknowingly predicted the sacrificial nature of the death of the Lord Jesus Christ, Pilate was also unknowingly proclaiming the unique quality of the **Prajāpati's Sacrifice.**

"Father, Forgive Them"

The sincere and sinless mind of Jesus was totally revealed on the cross when He said His last words. There was not even a little bit of hatred in His heart against the cruel people who severely treated Him and killed Him. He sincerely loved them even as He accepted mocking, spitting, whipping and nailing from them. He was not pretending to love them and was not following a philosophy or a doctrine. His action and words were coming from His unique personality. He is the embodiment of love and in Him there was no sin. That was the reason why He could pray for His enemies even at the time of His suffering on the cross. *"Father, forgive them, for they do not know what they are doing." (Luke 23:34).* This attitude of Jesus was a new message to the world. At the time of His public ministry, in the Sermon on the mount, He taught His disciples as follows: *"You have heard that it was said, 'Love your neighbor and hate your enemy.' But I tell you: Love your enemies and pray for those who persecute you, that you may be sons of your Father in heaven." (Matthew 5: 43-45)* Look at the credibility of the teaching of Jesus. What He taught, He practiced.

Why is the sinlessness of the Puruṣa so important in the sacrifice of Prajāpati? It is God's way of **Mukti or salvation.** By this sacrifice gods obtained heaven after the purification of their sin. We have seen earlier that these gods are the human beings who are born of **Ṛta** or sacrifice. The incarnated God offers Himself in the sacrifice. Only a God who is holy and sinless can reconcile man to Himself. "A Saviour not quite God would be like a bridge broken at the farthest end." Quoting this from Bishop Moule, Erwin W. Lutzer writes: "A Saviour who was less than God would be disqualified. God alone is able to save us."[72] When God came down from heaven He could not reject His holiness and sinlessness. Jesus, the **Puruṣa-Prajāpati,** was God and Man at the same time as portrayed in the **Puruṣasūkta.** Erwin W. Lutzer wrote, "His human and divine natures were united in one Person in such a way that it would be impossible for His humanity to sin without His deity being affected. For Christ's humanity to sin and His deity to remain sinless would set up an intolerable separation within the Person of Christ."[73]

"No man (sinner) can redeem the life of another or give to God a ransom for him." (Psalm 49:7) God, the sinless Man, is alone able to save us.

Result No. 1

What are the fruits of the sacrifice? Each characteristic of Christ's sacrifice has a corresponding result or fruit. What is the fruit when a sinless man gives Himself in sacrifice?

We already have the answer in the **Chāndogya Upaniṣad: "This Man (Puruṣa) is above all sins and one who worships (believes) Him and follows Him also raises himself above sin."**[74] Yes; the Man Christ Jesus came to save sinners from their sins. The sinless Man died as a sacrifice to make us sinless. St. John writes: *"The blood of Jesus, His Son, purifies us from all sin. Jesus Christ the Righteous One is the atoning sacrifice for our sins, and not only for ours but also for the sins of the whole world."* (1 John 1:10; 2:2)

The Brāhmaṇa Texts also give us the important outcome of the sacrifice as follows:

"By sacrifice people are freed from ANṚTA (SIN) from Varuṇa."[75]

Varuṇa is the ruler of the ocean. He has a **noose** in his hand and it is known as **Varuṇapāśam. By sacrifice man is freed from Varuṇa's noose.** In the Book of Revelation we see a ruler who is going to come from the sea and the Bible names him the **Beast.** (Revelation 13:1). The important result of the Puruṣa Prajāpati's sacrifice is to deliver us from Varuṇa's noose. The reason of the sacrifice was to destroy the devil's work and to give us freedom from sin. As the **Chāndogya Upaniṣad** says,

"As water does not stick on a lotus leaf so does an evil deed (sin) not stick to the man who knows this."[76]

The Apostle Paul's Testimony

St. Paul was a learned Jewish Rabbi who strongly opposed the early Christians and persecuted them. He wrote about the forgiveness of his sins as follows:

"Even though I was once a blasphemer and a persecutor and a violent man, I was shown mercy because I acted in ignorance and unbelief. The grace of the Lord was poured out on me abundantly, along with the faith and love that are in Christ Jesus. Here is a trustworthy saying that deserves full acceptance: Christ Jesus came into the world to save sinners - OF WHOM I AM WORST." (1.Timothy 1:13-15)

The Author's Testimony

This author also enjoys the fruits of the sacrifice since he believes in this Sacrifice. On December 19, 1970, I personally came to believe in this **Man Christ Jesus** who died for my sake. Before that, I was a slave of sin and I was always living under the fear of death. But from the moment that I believed in the Sacrifice of this perfect Man, Jesus, He took away all the burden and the fear of death from me and gave me the assurance of eternal life. He purified me with His own precious blood and gave me power to live a life free from sin. I was born again by the Spirit of the Lord and now His Spirit is living in me. As it is written, *"If anyone is in Christ Jesus, he is a new creation." (2.Cor. 5:17)*

The Fourth Stage of Sacrifice - A Living Sacrifice

In this fourth stage of sacrifice we are living in the sacrifice. Now we live in this world away from sin and *"offer our bodies as living sacrifices, holy and pleasing to God."* (Romans 12:1) St. Paul completes this verse saying, "This is our spiritual act of worship." In the Old Testament, Abraham considered the act of sacrifice to be worship. (Genesis 22:5) In fact, the New Testament-worship also centres around sacrifice and without sacrifice there is no worship. But now we don't have to offer bulls or goats in our worship. Those were mere symbols of Christ, the real Lamb of God who already was offered once for all according to the Scriptures. At present, we have to identify with the fruits of sacrifice. For that we have to imitate Jesus and love one another as Jesus loved us and gave Himself for each and every one of us. *"Live a life of love, just as Christ loved us and gave Himself up for us as a fragrant offering and sacrifice to God."* (Ephesians 5:2) Doing good, sharing with others and praising God constitute the continuing sacrifice in the period of the New Testament. The passage from the book of Hebrews illustrates it well: *"Through Jesus, therefore, let us continually offer to God a sacrifice of praise- the fruit of lips that confess His name. And do not forget to do good and share with others, for with such sacrifices God is pleased."* (Hebrews 13:15,16)

Share material wealth for the benefit of others and the work of the Lord becomes a living sacrifice. But whenever we give an offering to the Lord that offering should be holy and acceptable to God. God will not be pleased with our offering which is made through unholy means. God does not want money or any other form of wealth from sinners. Therefore, first of all man has to come to an assurance that his sin is completely forgiven through the perfect sacrifice of God. When we identify with the sacrificial **Puruṣa** we will be new creations. People who are newly created in the Lord Jesus are ordained to offer spiritual and living sacrifices everyday in the form of good works and the sharing of ourselves and whatever we have out of pure love for our Lord and Saviour Jesus Christ. True worship and praise come from the heart of such people.

Chapter 6

CHARACTERISTIC #2
THE CROWN OF THORNS

The Sacrificial Man has to be Completely Separated

In the **Puruṣasūkta** the Man is completely separated for the offering. **Śathapathabrāḥmaṇa** deals with the real man-sacrifice (**Puruṣa-medha**) on this earth which extends over five days. Here, the text says, man is seized and separated for the sacrifice on the central day.[77]

In the horse-sacrifice, we see that the horse is bound, bathed, consecrated near the fire and thus separated. We read about the ceremony of this separation in the thirteenth kāndha of the **Śathapathabrāḥmaṇa.** Sometimes they set apart the sacrificial animal by a crown made out of a creeping plant of the forest. This separated animal deserves no sympathy. It cannot be used for any other purpose. Once it is separated, it is separated for ever for the offering.

This feature is also fulfilled in Jesus' sacrifice. Jesus was completely separated for the eternal sacrifice. St. John recorded this as follows: *"The soldiers twisted together a crown of thorns and put it on His head. . .When Jesus came out wearing the crown of thorns and the purple robe, Pilate said to them,'Here is the MAN (PURUṢA)'."* (John 19:2,5) What a significant statement! Pilate was not a spiritual man and he was not even concerned about truth. But seeing the Man Jesus, as if the predictions in the Scriptures were known to him, he exclaimed,

'Here is the Man!'

We have seen that Caiaphas predicted His vicarious death even though he was not a real servant of God. In the same way God put words in the mouth of Pilate when he saw the features of the Prajāpati-Sacrifice in Jesus. Pilate was proclaiming to the world that the Man for the perfect sacrifice of God was ready to be offered. The next verse in the Gospel of John also supports this interpretation. *"As soon as the chief priests and their officials saw Him, they shouted, 'Crucify! Crucify!' " (verse 6)* In other words they said: "Sacrifice Him! Sacrifice Him! He is the real sacrifice!"

Jesus Knew that He was Separated

From His childhood Jesus knew that He was separated for the supreme sacrifice. When He was twelve years old, at the time of the Feast of Passover in the Jerusalem temple where Joseph and Mary missed Jesus for three days, Jesus asked them:

"Didn't you know I had to be in my Father's house?" (Luke:2:49)

"But", as St. Luke records it, "they did not understand what He was saying to them." (verse.50) At the beginning of His public ministry, John the Baptist who baptized Him in water proclaimed: "Look! The Lamb of God, who takes away the sins of the world!" (John 1:29). Through the act of passive obedience to His water baptism Jesus was telling the whole world that He was the sacrificial Lamb of God who was fully separated for that sacrifice alone. At that moment heaven was opened and a voice was heard: *"This is my Son whom I love; with Him I am well pleased."* (Matthew 3:17) At the time of His forty days fast He was alone in the desert where He was preparing for His sacrificial ministry knowing that He was fully separated for the sacrifice. When we analyze His teachings and actions we can easily understand that through out His ministry He was heading in the one and only direction that led to His sacrifice. Jesus was single-minded towards the culmination of the sacrifice because He was separated for that purpose alone. When the appointed time came the sacrificers twisted together a crown of thorns and put it on His head. Thus He was properly sealed and separated for the perfect sacrifice.

Result #2

What is the corresponding fruit of this feature; the wearing of a crown of thorns and being separated? The people of the world will give a crown to every believer and isolate him from them. They will insult and persecute him. Jesus warned the believers: "You will be hated by all nations because of Me." (Matthew 24:9) "If the world hates you, keep in mind that it hated Me first. If you belonged to the world, it would love you as its own. As it is you do not belong to the world, but I have chosen you out of the world. That is why the world hates you. Remember the words I spoke to you: 'No servant is greater than his master.' If they persecuted Me they will persecute you also." (John 15:18-20) When this world begins to give you a crown of thorns you have to understand that you are completely separated for the living sacrifice. You also have to be aware that you deserve no sympathy because you are appointed for that purpose.

For the believer, wearing the crown of thorns is a great privilege since he is identifying with the various aspects of the great sacrifice. The believer considers the cross of Christ greater than the riches of the world.

St. Paul's Testimony

"For Your sake we face death all day long; we are considered as sheep to be slaughtered." (Romans 8:36)

"I have been in prison more frequently, been flogged more severely and been exposed to death again and again.... (2 Cor. 11:23)
". . .or Christ's sake I delight...in insults, in hardships, in persecutions, in difficulties." (2.Cor.12:10)

Richard Wurmbrand says:

Richard Wurmbrand suffered fourteen years of Communist imprisonment and torture in his homeland of Rumania for Christ's sake.

Once Richard was asked in prison:

"Do you believe that God created man in His own image?"

"I certainly do" he said

"Do you believe that you are the image of God?"

"Of course" He said.

Immediately the officer who asked these questions took a mirror out of his pocket and handed it to him and said: "Look into the glass. See how ugly you are. You have dark circles under your eyes. You are all skin and bones. Your whole appearance is haggard, like a madman. If you are in the image of God, God must be as ugly as you are. Why should you worship Him?"

"Yes, my God has an ugly face like me." Giving answer to the officer Wurmbrand writes, "We saw this face on Golgotha. His hair was disordered, His brow was disfigured by wounds. Spittle and blood mingled on His face. He had dark circles under His eyes. 'He had no form nor comeliness.' "[78] This Man wore a crown of thorns on His head and from there blood was channeling through His face. Pointing out the importance of identification with the sacrifice, Wurmbrand writes: "Everyone who suffers bears the image of God who became `a man of sorrows and acquainted with grief.'"[79]

As a personal testimony I can say that the Lord allowed the world to give me the crown of thorns and taught me to be thankful to them who offered me the crown . Through many events I could see the power of God and the victory of the sacrifice. St. Peter exhorts us: *"Rejoice that you participate in the suffering of Christ, so that you may be overjoyed when His glory is revealed. If you are insulted because of the name of Christ, you are blessed for the spirit of glory and of God rests on you."* (1.Peter 4:13,14)

Be Separated For Good Works and Sharing

In the fourth stage of the sacrifice we consider ourselves to be separated for good works and sharing which are the continuation of the New Testament sacrifices and worship. Since we are separated and ordained for doing good to others we have no other choice. When we decide to offer a sacrifice of sharing our material blessings, first of all we have to separate that part willingly. Once you separate it do not take it back. Reject it, sacrifice it, and the results will be seen later.

Chapter 7

CHARACTERISTIC #3
THE REJECTION

The sacrificial victim should be rejected by His own people

Rejection by our own people is really painful. Many of us may have experienced this bitter agony to some extent but we often forget that by this we are identifying with the characteristics of the eternal sacrifice of God.

Without the rejection, the third characteristic of the Prajāpati-sacrifice, the sacrifice would not have been performed. First of all, this rejection happened in heaven in the **Man's Sacrifice**. In the **Puruṣasūkta** when the **devas** sacrificed **the Puruṣa**, God - the Father - was silent. We can find this feature in the animal sacrifice which is the second stage of the sacrifice. G. Suseelan makes reference to this in the **Itareya Brāḥmaṇa** in the context suggested by this translation: **"The sacrificial animal should be rejected by its father, mother, brother, sister and friends."** [80] The animal has to be completely abandoned and separated for the sacrifice. This is exactly fulfilled in Jesus. St. John wrote about this:

"He came to that which was His own, but His own did not receive Him." (John 1:11)

Representing the Jewish community, their high priests officially rejected Him on the day of Preparation of Passover Week in front of Pilate, the Roman Governor. When Jesus, the King of the Jews and the King of kings, came to offer Himself up as the sacrifice, Pilate said to the Jews:

"Here is your king."

But they shouted, "Take Him away! Take Him away! Crucify Him!"

"Shall I crucify your king?" Pilate asked.

"We have no king but Caesar," the chief priests answered.

St. John concluded this portion as follows:

"Finally Pilate handed Him over to them to be crucified." (John 19:14-16)

In the Old Testament the Prophet Isaiah also predicted the rejection of the suffering Servant, the Man of sorrows:

"He was despised and rejected by men.. . . (Isaiah 53:3)

As He was led like a Lamb to the slaughter almost all of His disciples deserted Him. Judas betrayed Him and Peter disowned Him three times. Jesus Christ Himself pointed out this rejection on the Passover night as follows:

"This very night you will all fall away on account of Me, for it is written: 'I will strike the shepherd, and the sheep of the flock will be scattered'." (Matthew 26:31)

His own brothers and family members did not come forward and they also rejected Him. They could not understand His teachings. The Gospel of John says,

"Even His own brothers did not believe on Him." (John 7:5) St.Mark quotes His family members as saying,

"He is out of His mind." (Mark 3:21)

The rejection was completed when the heavenly Father forsook Him on the cross. On the cross Jesus cried out in a loud voice,

"Eloi,Eloi, lama sabchthani?" which means,**"My God, My God, why have you forsaken Me?"** (Matthew 27:46)

About 1000 years before this, through King David Psalm 22 was written as a prophecy of the sacrificial death of the Lord Jesus Christ. The first verse of the Psalm is this: "My God, my God, why have you forsaken me?" Isaiah also wrote in advance that it was the LORD'S (Father's) will to crush Him. (Isaiah 53:10). We have seen in the **Purusasukta** that the Almighty God was silent when the **devas** sacrificed the **Man (Purusa).**

Result No. 3

When you believe in this sacrifice the sacrifice is yours. If you want your life to bear fruit, you have to identify with the sacrifice. It is painful but the Lord will give you grace to suffer that cross. Before you bear the fruit of the sacrifice, you have to be rejected by your own close friends, brothers and sisters and relatives.

A true believer has to go down this difficult and narrow way. Jesus said:

"Brother will betray brother to death, and a father his child; children will rebel against their parents and have them put to death. All men will hate you because of Me, but he who stands firm to the end will be saved. . . a man's enemies will be the members of his own household. Anyone who loves his father or mother more than Me is not worthy of Me; anyone who loves his son or daughter more than Me is not worthy of Me; and anyone who does not take his cross and follow me is not worthy of Me." (Matt.10:21,22 37,38).

What are the fruits of suffering? We share the love of Jesus. We will learn how to love our persecutors as Jesus loved and prayed for His enemies: "Father, forgive them for they do not know what they are doing." (Luke 23:34) We learn endurance. In every respect we will be identifying with Jesus. Jesus said, "If a man abides in Me and I in him, he will bear much fruit." (John 15:5). When we do not have any bitterness against anybody, our hearts will be filled with joy, peace, patience, kindness and goodness. These are the fruits of sacrifice. On the other hand, if we do not forgive our enemies our hearts will be filled with envy and bitterness. This attitude is destructive. Dealing with the seven deadly sins Dr. Anthony Campolo writes,"Envy is the major cause of unhappiness and self-contempt. Those who envy are never happy with what they are and have."[81]

St. Paul's testimony

When St. Paul started to follow Jesus he experienced this rejection from his own community. As soon as he started his preaching ministry the Jews - his own people - made plans to kill him. "Day and night they kept close watch on the city gates **in order to kill him.**" (Acts 9:24) On another occasion, forty Jewish men (his own people) formed a conspiracy and bound themselves with an oath not to eat or drink until they had killed Paul. (Acts 23:12)

St.Paul even experienced this rejection from the Christian believers. At the closing of his ministry he wrote to Timothy:

"You know every one in the province of Asia has deserted me, including Phygelus and Hermogenes." (2.Timothy 1:15)

At the end of the letter he wrote: *"At my first defense, no one came to my support, but everyone deserted me. May it not be held against them.*" (2. Timothy 4:16) The great Apostle Paul was rejected by his own people in this period of his life time. In this rejection we see one of the important aspects of the Prajapati-Sacrifice as well as its fulfillment. When we are forsaken by our friends and relatives we must not be dismayed. Remember, we are identifying with the **Man (Puruṣa) who was rejected by His own people** and who gave Himself for us in the perfect sacrifice.

From the Autobiography of Pastor K. E. Abraham

Pastor K. E. Abraham is known as one of the apostles of India in the twentieth century. The Holy Spirit used him mightily. His 500 page autobiography still testifies to this truth even after his death. He is the founder of the India Pentecostal Church, the largest Pentecostal movement in India. He possessed a charismatic Christian personality. However, he too was rejected for a certain period by his own close friends who were also real believers. A short description of it can be seen in his autobiography.[82] The people who were blessed by his own ministry stood against him. They used many sharp weapons against him but our heavenly father protected him by divine grace.

The Author's Testimony

This author was also fortunate to be rejected by his own people for a certain period of his life time. But the Lord was teaching him lessons of sacrifice through that experience. During this period he got enough time to write this book. Praise God. "And we know that in all things God works for good to those who love Him, who have been called according to his purpose." (Romans 8:28)

The Sacrificial Rejection and the Divine Protection

The victim of the sacrifice is always protected by God even though he is rejected by all. The thirteenth **kāṇdha** of the **Śathapath-abrāḥmaṇa** deals with the famous **Áśvamedha** (Horse Sacrifice). In this horse sacrifice the horse which is going to be sacrificed is left alone to wander for a year. But the powerful king who performs this sacrifice employs armed soldiers for the protection of the horse which is completely separated for the sacrifice.[83] If anybody dares to do any harm to the horse the king will annihilate him along with his family. Therefore the sacrificial horse is completely protected.

This rejection and divine protection can be seen in the Old Testament typologies of Christ's sacrifice such as the sacrifice of Isaac in the book of Genesis. [84] Isaac was rejected and separated for the sacrifice by his Father Abraham just as Jesus was by His own Father in heaven. Isaac was divinely protected and spared, but at the same time the sacrifice was done in the sight of God. Joseph, another shadow of the sacrificial Man Jesus Christ in the Old Testament, was also rejected by all his brothers, but at the same time God saved him miraculously, protected him and exalted him in His time. But for Jacob, his father, Joseph was dead for many years as Jacob saw his robe stained with blood. He did not know a goat was slain for Joseph and thus he was spared. However, in the end, Jacob received Joseph as if he were resurrected from the dead (Genesis 38) Another prophet of God, Moses, was also rejected by His own people until the appointed time of God. The Martyr Stephen mentioned this in his last sermon, as follows:

"This is the same Moses whom they had rejected with the words,'who made you ruler and judge?' He was sent to be their ruler and deliverer by God Himself." (Acts 7:35)

And we know that Moses' life was a sacrifice for his own people. The sacrifice of Christ was the fulfillment of all that was foreshadowed by these examples of rejection and divine protection. Remember, if you are identifying with Christ's sufferings, you are fully protected by Almighty God at the time of your rejection. For God says to us:

"Fear not, for I have redeemed you. . . When you pass through the waters, I will be with you. When you walk through the rivers, they will not sweep over you. When you walk through the fire, you will not be burned; the flames will not set you ablaze. . . Since you are precious and honored in my sight, and because I love you, I will give men in exchange for you, . . . " (Isaiah 43:1-4)

Self-Rejection: The Fourth Stage of Sacrifice

In the New Testament worship when we come to offer the spiritual sacrifice we too have to be rejected by ourselves. Self is the greatest enemy who works against us in producing the fruit of sacrifice. When we start doing good, sharing ourselves and our wealth with the needy and praising God, the New Testament ways of sacrifice, immediately the Self will say:

"You are a fool. Why do you sacrifice yourself?" An ordinary man does not have answers for this question. He keeps on loving himself and therefore he is unable to offer his life as a living sacrifice. The mysterious result of sacrifice is revealed only through Jesus who denied Himself and sacrificed His life for us. Jesus said to His disciples,

"If any one would come after me, he must deny himself and take up his cross daily and follow me." (Luke 9:23)

It is very difficult to understand that we have to deny ourselves in order to follow Jesus and worship Him. The desire of the self is not always good.

When I start to walk in the path of God my 'self' will not agree with my spirit. I know in my spirit that the desire of the'self' is not good for me. Therefore I must sacrifice the desire of the 'self'. I know the desire of my 'self' leads me to eternal destruction while the Word of God leads me to eternal life.

In the same way we have to sacrifice many other precious things: traditions and our pet opinions which are against the Word of God. When you start to follow the path of God, sometimes you have to face great opposition from your own father, mother, sisters, and brothers or your own wife or husband. But Jesus says,

"Anyone who loves his father or mother more than me is not worthy of me; anyone who loves his son or daughter more than me is not worthy of me; and anyone who does not take his cross and follow me is not worthy of me." (Matthew 10:37) To deny ourselves and take up the cross is the beginning of the living sacrifice. Jesus reveals the mystery of the sacrifice in the next verse: *"Who ever finds his life will lose it, and whoever loses his life for my sake will find it."* (verse 39) Pointing out His own sacrificial death which was going to happen Jesus explained the mystery of sacrifice as follows: *"I tell you the truth, unless a kernel of wheat falls to the ground and dies, it remains only a single seed. But if it dies it produces many seeds. The man who loves his life will lose it, while the man who hates his life in this world will keep it for eternal life."* (John 12:24,25) In the same way we have to reject our 'self' in order that we too, may fall to the ground and be sacrificed. Then we will see the multiple results of sacrifice. Surely it produces many seeds.

Rejection in the Sacrifice of Giving

In the same way, when we are determined in our hearts to make an offering to God from our material blessings, as the first step, we have to separate it as we noticed in the last chapter. The second step is to reject it. Offer all the wealth that you have separated willingly and cheerfully. Concerning the matter of giving, the Holy Bible says: "Each man should give what he has decided in his heart to give, not reluctantly or under compulsion, **for God loves a cheerful giver.**" (2 Cor.9:7) "For if the willingness is there, the gift is acceptable according to what one has, not according to what he does not have." (2 Cor.8:12)

When you do the sacrifice of giving give it with a cheerful spirit. If you want to give it cheerfully you have to separate it and reject it in your heart. This kind of giving is the acceptable sacrifice to God without which there can be no worship according to the New Testament. The economic principle of God is equality. St Paul writes: *". . . there might be equality. At the present time your plenty will supply what they need, so that in turn their plenty will supply what you need. Then there will be equality, as it is written: He who gathered much did not have too much, and he who gathered little did not have too little.* (2.Cor.13-15)

Prosperity is the immediate result of the sacrifice of giving. The **Brāḥmaṇa Texts** deal with material blessings as the result of performing sacrifice.

The 13th **kāndha** of the **Śathapathabrāḥmaṇa** describes various results of the horse-sacrifice.[85] Along with the forgiveness of sin, food, many children, wealth, cattle, victory over enemies, fame and all kinds of prosperity are the results of the **Áśvamedha (Horse sacrifice).**

God promises financial blessing and prosperity to the New Testament believer along with persecution and the cross. Jesus says, "I tell you the truth, no one who has left home or brothers or sisters or mother or father or children or fields for me and the gospel will fail to receive a hundred times as much in this present age (homes, brothers, sisters, mothers, children and fields-and with them, persecutions) and in the age to come, eternal life." (Mark 10:29,30)

The principle in the mystery of the sacrifice of giving is this:"A man reaps what he sows." (Galatians 6:7) Therefore as St Paul writes, *"Whoever sows sparingly will also reap sparingly, and whoever sows generously will also reap generously."* (2.Cor. 9:6) Having full assurance of faith a farmer separates the best of his seeds and at the appointed time he most willingly rejects them and throws them in the muddy ground. Sowing is a sacrifice but harvest is its glorious result. This is the established principle of sacrifice:

"Those who sow in tears will reap with songs of joy. He who goes out weeping, carrying seed to sow, will return with songs of joy, carrying sheaves with him." (Psalm 126:5,6)

Is it not an amazing revelation that all these features of the **Prajāpati-sacrifice** which originated in the heart of the Almighty God have a direct link to all the four stages of sacrifice? These features were continued in the animal sacrifice in its second stage and they were fulfilled in the Lord Jesus Christ in His perfect sacrifice on the cross. They are 'fruited' in the believers in its final stage.

Chapter 8

CHARACTERISTIC #4

THE SILENT SUFFERER

The Sacrificial Man should be a silent Sufferer

This is the next feature of this glorious sacrifice. Here, we see that **Puruṣa-Prajāpati** silently gives Himself in this great offering. The words of the **Ṛg Veda** describe so well the attitude of the **Man:**

> **"Like a horse I have yoked myself - well knowing to the pole. I seek neither release nor turning back."[86]**

At the appointed time Jesus surrendered Himself into the hands of the soldiers telling them, **"I am He."** Most willingly He gave Himself to be sacrificed. When Peter began to fight against His arrest Jesus commanded him "Put your sword away! Shall I not drink the cup the Father has given me."[87]

In the Vedas, the person who kills the sacrificial animal is called **śamitāra** which means **silencer.** His job is to make the animal calm. In order to make him calm he asks the animal to be quiet. We have references in the **Taittirīya Saṃhita** and in the **Āpastamba śrutasūtraṃ.**[88] However, it is an important characteristic encountered in the Prajāpati-Sacrifice. This is fulfilled in Jesus in its strictest sense. About 700 years before the birth of the Lord Jesus Christ, the prophet Isaiah predicted this in the Servant's Song:

"He was oppressed and afflicted, yet He did not open His mouth; He was led like a lamb to the slaughter, and as a sheep before her shearers is silent, so He did not open His mouth." (Isaiah 53:7)

Before the Sanhedrin when false accusations came against Him, Jesus remained silent and gave no answer. (Mark 14:55-61) Jesus did not try to defend Himself even before Pilate, the Roman governor. At one point Pilate asked Him, **"Do you refuse to speak to me?"** (John 19:10) Yes, Jesus the Lamb of God, the sinless and perfect victim in the perfect sacrifice, was the perfect silent sufferer at the time of His sacrifice.

Result No. 4

To bear fruit of the sacrifice we have to share the sacrifice. We have to learn to face false accusation and to carry our cross without any complaint. Rev. Robert J. Daly quotes the opinion of Origen, one of the early church fathers, about sharing the sacrifice of the Lord Jesus Christ: "Origin sees prayer, forgiveness, almsgiving and good works as the fruit of sacrifice."[89] Only a silent sufferer can forgive his enemies and still continue to bear fruit of the sacrifice with great patience and blessed hope.

The Author's Testimony

Hereby, I confess myself to be incapable of being a silent sufferer. How often have I raised my voice when problems arose. I tried to prove my position when accusations came against me. I wanted to convince other people that I was innocent. I could not suffer the cross silently. I talked to my close friends but none felt sympathy for the sacrificial animal. Here, the Lord taught me a lesson:

A sacrificial animal has no right to complain. He should be silent. But often we try to defend ourselves and make petitions to the Lord: "O Lord, take it away from me." The Lord's answer is always this:

"My grace is sufficient for you, for my power is made perfect in weakness." (2.Cor.12:9) When we are willingly enduring the agonies of rejection from our relatives and friends, we are identifying with the features of the **Prajāpati-sacrifice.** Through many experiences the Lord will teach us to suffer the cross silently. There we can completely identify with the eternal sacrifice of God.

The Silent Giver

In the fourth stage of sacrifice, when we follow the path of sacrificial giving it has to be silent. All good works which are the fruits of sacrifice have to be performed out of pure love of God and for the glory of God. Jesus taught us this principle in these words:

"Be careful not do your 'acts of righteousness' before men, to be seen by them. If you do, you will have no reward from your Father in heaven. So when you give to the needy do not announce it with trumpets, as the hypocrites do in the synagogues and on the streets, to be honored by men. I tell you the truth, they have received their reward in full. But when you give to the needy, do not let your left hand know what your right hand is doing, so that your giving may be in secret. Then your Father, who sees what is done in secret, will reward you." (Matthew 6:1-4)

Chapter 9

CHARACTERISTIC #5
CLOSE TO THE CROSS

The Sacrificial animal should be closely tied to the sacrificial pillar

The use of the sacrificial post to which the victim is tied is an essential part of the sacrifice. In his book, The Vedic and the Christian Concept of Sacrifice Fr. Jose Thachil quotes numerous portions from the Brāhmaṇa texts in order to point out the divine origin of the **yūpa** - the sacrificial post. The importance of the sacrificial pillar is emphasised in the Brāhmana texts. Fr. Thachil quotes from the **Śathapatha brāhmaṇa** as follows:

"Na va ṛte yupāt paśum ālabhante kadācana."
(Never do they immolate an animal without a sacrificial post.)[90]

We cannot find such a clear restriction concerning the sacrificial pillar in the Old Testament sacrifices. Still we read from the book of Psalms: "Bind the sacrifice with cords, even unto the horns of the altar."(Psalm 118:27) Binding the sacrificial animal is essential to perform any kind of sacrifice. In the sacrifice of the **Man** in the **Puruṣasūkta** we see the **Puruṣa** is also tied to the sacrificial post. Verse 15 of the **Sūkta** ends this way:

"Devā yadyajñaṃ tanvāna abadhnan puruṣaṃ paśuṃ."

(The devas who performed this sacrifice tied Puruṣa, the sacrificial animal.)

In the commentary of the **Puruṣasūkta, Sayanacarya** writes as follows:

"Yajñaṃ yajñasādhanabhūtam taṃ Puruṣaṃ paśutvabhāvanaya yupe baddhaṃ..."[91]

Here the **Puruṣa** is pictured as the victim of sacrifice who is tied to the sacrificial post like an animal. As we have seen above from the **Ṛg Veda,** He had yoked Himself to the pole like a horse. He sought neither release nor turning back.

The Cross was the sacrificial post of the Lord Jesus Christ. About the crucifixion St. John writes:

"Carrying His own cross, He went out to the place of the Skull (which in Aramaic is called Golgotha). Here they crucified Him, and with Him two others- one on each side and Jesus in the middle." (John 19:17,18)

And so were brought to a climax the activities of the redemptive sacrifice.

Result No. 5

Although the sacrificial post is insignificant in the Old Testament, the cross is the vital part of the New Testament. This is plainly stated by Leon Morris, "In the New Testament, salvation centres on the cross."[92] In fact, the cross is the foundation of the Christian faith. Before the crucifixion of the Lord, the cross was the emblem of shame and reproach as it is written, "Cursed is everyone who is hung on a tree." From the Old Testament scriptures, this portion is quoted by St. Paul in the book of Galatians in connection with the death of Jesus Christ.[93] In this context it is worthy to be noted that the **Brāhmaṇa texts** give much importance and sanctity to the post even before the crucifixion of the Lord.

According to the Vedic texts, the fruit of the sacrifice is to come through the post and therefore the ancients were very conscientious in selecting the tree for the **yūpa.** Their prosperity, splendour, health and the forgiveness of sins were dependent upon the sacrificial post. Quoting from the **Brāhmaṇa texts**, Fr. Jose Thachil writes:

"The **Aitareya Brāhmaṇa** says the sacrificial post is a thunderbolt. **It stands erect as a weapon against the foe.** Similarly the **Kausītaki-Brāhmaṇa** says:'the sacrificial post is a thunderbolt. In that they erect the post on the fast day, *verily thus with a thunderbolt they smite away the evil of the sacrificer.' Thus the yupa works* **against the enemy, the evil spirits, etc."**[94] The sacrificer or the believer of the sacrifice achieves victory over sin and the devil by means of the sacrifice of the Perfect Man Jesus on the cross. Therefore the sacrificial post - the cross - is the symbol of the complete and ultimate victory over satanic forces. St. Paul wrote in Colossians:

"When you were dead in your sins and in the uncircumcision of your sinful nature, God made you alive with Christ. He forgave us all our sins, having canceled the written code, with its regulations, that was against us and that stood opposed to us; He took it away, nailing it to the CROSS. And having disarmed the powers and authorities, He made a public spectacle of them, triumphing over them by the CROSS." (Col.2:13-15)

Surely the cross is the thunderbolt with which the believer of the sacrifice can smite away sin and its author, Satan.

A believer has to share the cross of the Lord Jesus Christ for victory over sin and the devil. He needs deliverance from his old sinful nature. As Watchman Nee writes, "We need forgiveness for what we have done, but we need deliverance from what we are. Objectively, therefore, the blood delivers us from the power of the enemy,. . . while subjectively the cross delivers us by dealing with the flesh, the ground of the enemy's activity in us. The blood can wash away my sins, but it cannot wash away my 'old man'. I need the cross to crucify me the sinner."[95]

That is the reason why the Lord Jesus said, "*anyone who does not take his cross and follow me is not worthy of Me.*" (Matthew 10:38) The apostle Paul wrote, "Those who belong to Christ Jesus have crucified the sinful nature with its passions and desires." (Gal.5:24) St. Paul writes in the book of Romans, "Therefore, I urge you, brothers, in view of God's mercy, to offer your bodies as living sacrifices, holy and pleasing to God - this is your spiritual act of worship. Do not conform any longer to the pattern of this world, but be transformed by the renewing of your mind." (Romans 12:1,2.)

As the author's testimony I also witness that the cross delivered me from my old self and now I am in the process of transformation.

The Living Sacrifice Through the Cross

In the fourth stage of sacrifice we discover a very important point concerning the matter of giving and doing good in connection with the sacrificial pillar - cross. We do not have any goodness in ourselves. Whatever goodness we have is inherited by us through the cross - through the sacrifice of Jesus Christ.

Therefore whatever good thing we do, we do through the cross of Jesus. The offering has to be placed before the altar . The altar is greater than the offering. (Matthew 23: 18-20) In the New Testament-sacrifice the cross is the altar. When we give to the needy ones, do it through the love of the cross of Jesus. Bring your sacrifice to the altar. The altar will make your gifts sacred. (Matthew 23:19) That is the proper way of giving and then it will be beneficial to the giver and the recipients.

Chapter 10

CHARACTERISTIC #6
THE BLOOD

The blood of the sacrificial Man should be shed

The shedding of blood is the essence of the sacrifice. After having studied the Old Testament sacrifices in the light of their fulfillment in the crucifixion, the author of the book of Hebrews makes this declaration:

"Without shedding blood there is no forgiveness." (Hebrews 9:22).

Even though there is no direct verse indicating bloodshed in the **Sacrifice of the Man** in the **Puruṣasūkta,** it is obvious that there was bloodshed and without it, it would have been impossible to complete the sacrifice. However, we have seen this **Man who was bruised** in the **Bṛhadāraṇyaka Upaniṣad.**

There we see that **blood was flowing from Him just like sap oozes from the cut tree.**[96]

That tree is the **Áśvattha tree**, the inverted tree which came down from heaven that we have seen in the second chapter.

Even though bloodshed is the most important part of the sacrifice, one may feel it is horrible and senseless. But if we go deeply into the subject and see the fulfillment of the bloodshed, we will be amazed to see its significance. Blood means life. The Lord God says in the Holy Bible:

"For the life of a creature is in the blood, and I have given it (the animal's blood) to you to make atonement for one's life." (Levi.17:11)

Christ's hands and legs were nailed to the cross, the sacrificial pillar, and by His own blood He made atonement for our lives. That was the perfect and complete sacrifice, and it never has to be repeated. As it is written,

"He did not enter by means of the blood of goats and calves; but He entered the Most Holy Place once for all by His own blood, having obtained eternal redemption." (Hebrews 9:12) Even the last drop of His blood was poured out in the crucifixion. St.John, who was an eyewitness of the crucifixion, recorded the completeness of the blood-sacrifice as follows:

"One of the soldiers pierced Jesus' side with a spear, bringing a sudden flow of blood and water. The man who saw it has given testimony, and his testimony is true. He knows that he tells the truth, and he testifies so that you also may believe." (John 19:34,35)

Jesus bled until the last drop of His blood had left His body. St. John records this truth with the great intention that everybody should believe in Jesus. Under the influence of the Holy Spirit, John was proclaiming the shedding of blood, the very important feature of the Prajāpati-sacrifice, which was fulfilled in Jesus' crucifixion.

Result No. 6

The fruit of the shed blood of Jesus is the full benefit of salvation. First of all, the blood gives us life. We were dead in our sins because the wages of sin is death. But in our place, Jesus died and paid the penalty in full. Through His blood we live forever. Inviting us to believe in His sacrifice, Jesus figuratively says: "*Whoever eats my flesh and drinks my blood has eternal life, and I will raise him up* at *the last day.*" (John 6:54) Jesus destroyed the power of death by His own blood and delivered us from the fear of death.

"The blood of Jesus purifies us from all our sins." (1.John 1:7)

Everyday we need this blood for the cleansing of our soul and spirit, just like we require the circulation of blood in our body for purifying all the impurities in the body. Before we were saved by the shedding of Jesus' blood, all encounters between God and man were hostile. A holy God does not tolerate sin. With sin nobody could stand before God. Even to Moses, the great servant of God, the vision of God was so terrifying that Moses said, "I am trembling with fear." (Hebrews:12:21) But now, we have an advocate "who speaks to the Father in our defense - Jesus Christ, the Righteous One. He is the atoning sacrifice for our sins." (1.John 2:1)

Now, we are able to go into the presence of the Lord at any time to worship Him. He re-established fellowship between man and God through shedding His own blood and **for this reason Christ is the mediator of the new covenant.** He renewed the covenant by His own blood. That is why Jesus said in the last supper, **"This cup is the new covenant in my BLOOD."** (1.Cor.11:25)

As it is written, "God presented Him as a sacrifice of atonement, through faith in His blood." (Romans 3:25) "God was pleased to have all His fullness dwell in Him, and through Him to reconcile to Himself all things, whether things on earth or things in heaven, by making peace through His blood, shed on the cross." (Colossians 1:19,20).

Thus Jesus, the Son of God and the Son of Man (**Puruṣa-Prajāpati,** offers the new covenant of peace and forgiveness to mankind, written not in ink but in His own precious blood. Therefore, make sure to receive His offer of covenant with a full heart.

"How shall we escape if we ignore such a great salvation?" (Hebrews 2:3)

The Shedding of Blood in the Living Sacrifice

What is the significance of the shed-blood in the fourth stage of sacrifice? We do not have any bloodshed in this New Testament period. The blood of Jesus Christ which He shed in the eternal sacrifice is still effective. Therefore today the blood of Christ empowers us to offer living and acceptable sacrifices of praise and good works. Nothing good lives in our 'self'. Therefore, to produce the fruit of sacrifice our old self has to die. Bloodshed means death. When we identify with the shed-blood of Jesus we identify with the death of

Jesus. It means our old self died with Christ. "All of us who were baptized into Christ Jesus were baptized into His death." (Romans 6:3) We have to "count ourselves dead to sins and alive to God in Christ Jesus" (Romans 6:11) through His resurrection in order to offer a living sacrifice.

Bleeding is always a serious matter. In the same way we have to consider the fruit of the sacrifice to be very serious. We have to do good seriously and conscientiously trusting in the power of the blood of Jesus.

Chapter 11

CHARACTERISTIC # 7
THE BONES

The Sacrificial Man's bones should not be broken

This is a very important and notable feature of almost all the animal sacrifices related to the **Prajāpati-sacrifice.** We have a fine description of this in the **Brāḥmana Texts.**

The Itareya Brāḥmaṇa prescribes that the sacrificer separate the twenty six ribs of the animal carefully without breaking them.[97]

In the book of Exodus in the Old Testament we have the command not to break the bones of the sacrificial lamb of the Passover. The verse specifically says:

"Do not break any of the bones." (Exodus 12:46)

"For Christ, our Passover lamb, has been sacrificed." (1.Cor.5:7) Thus St. Paul connects Christ with the Passover lamb in the New Testament. Fulfilling this feature, none of the bones of Jesus were broken even though He was literally crushed on the cross, the sacrificial post. St.John records in his Gospel as follows:

"Now it was the day of Preparation, and the next day was to be a special Sabbath. Because the Jews did not want the bodies left on the crosses during the Sabbath, they asked Pilate to have the legs broken and the bodies taken down. The soldiers therefore came and broke the legs of the first man who had been crucified with Jesus, and

then those of the others. But when they came to Jesus and found that He was already dead, THEY DID NOT BREAK HIS LEGS. . .The man who saw it has given testimony, and his testimony is true. . .These things happened so that the scripture would be fulfilled: "Not one of His bones will be broken." (John 19:31-36)

See how miraculously the features of the Prajāpati-Sacrifice are fulfilled in the crucifixion of the Lord Jesus Christ.

Result no. 7

What is the corresponding result of this characteristic with the eternal sacrifice? We have seen that we are sharing the fruit of the sacrifice when we believe in it. We have a key in the Book of Psalms to open the door of this revelation:

"A righteous man may have many troubles, but the Lord delivers him from them all; He protects all his bones, not one of them will be broken." (Psalm 34:19)

Bones (skeleton) are the support or protective framework of a human or animal body. The outside structure must conform to the nature of the fundamental framework of the bones inside. God strictly forbad the breaking of any bone of the sacrificial animal. In the sacrifice of Jesus, God preserved all His bones intact and so protected the essential nature of the human body. God didn't allow anyone to break any of them. But His body was broken on the cross. In the same way, when we share the fellowship of the sacrifice of the Lord Jesus Christ, God allows our outward bodies to be broken but He will keep us alive fundamentally and eternally. Troubles may be many but He will deliver us from all of them and he will protect all our bones.

What a great relief to know that we are safe when we share the blessed sacrifice of the Lord.

St. Paul's Testimony

The testimony of St. Paul is relevant in this context: *"We are hard pressed on every side, but not crushed; perplexed, but not in despair; persecuted, but not abandoned; struck down, but not de-*

stroyed. We always carry around in our body the death of Jesus, so that the life of Jesus may also be revealed in our body." (2.Cor. 4 8-10)

The Author's Testimony

I glorify the Lord along with all other true believers for His protection and preservation. God has a definite plan for my life and that plan is the bone structure or the skeleton which is the protective framework of the external body. Nobody can destroy God's plan for your life even though you have to go through the painful experience of being persecuted and hard pressed. You may be pressed but you will not be crushed. God's eternal plan will be fulfilled.

The Unbroken Bones in the Living Sacrifice

The unbroken bones are full of meaning in the fourth stage of the living sacrifice. As we offer a sacrifice of giving to the work of the Lord we are responsible to preserve all its 'bones'. The sacrificer has to give account to the Lord. Do not waste even a cent which was separated for the sacrifice of giving.

Chapter 12

CHARACTERISTIC #8
THE MAN ALIVE

The Sacrificial Victim of the Prajāpati-Sacrifice should Return to Life After the Sacrifice

The sacrificial victim, the **Puruṣa** in the **Puruṣasūkta,** becomes alive even after His sacrificial death. Hereafter, the **Puruṣa** shines forth as the eternal shelter of mankind and the purpose of all creation. The **Puruṣa** is not annihilated by the sacrifice. The work of **Puruṣa** did not finish there. Scholars in this field usually call this: "The reconstruction of Prajāpati's body." We have already noticed in the first chapter that the world was created as the primary result of the Man-sacrifice in the **Puruṣasūkta. The Śathapatha Brāḥmaṇa** also describes how **Prajāpati** dismembered Himself to create the world. The verse concludes with the description of the complete restoration of the body of **Prajāpati.**[98]

H. Aguilar quotes from **Aitareya Āraṇyaka** in this way: **"Prajāpati put Himself together again by means of the chandas, the Word-the Scriptures ."** [99]

Introducing the bruised **Man** who was dying, dripping blood like sap from the cut-tree, the **Bṛhadāraṇyaka Upaniṣad asks:**

"After the Puruṣa was cut off by death,
from which root does He comes forth?"

The text itself gives us the answer in the next verse:

"But the Puruṣa lives again." (More details in the Endnote.)[100]

Some scholars think that this reconstruction story of the **Prajāpati's** body is a myth and this type of sacrifice has not yet been made on earth.

But this important feature is fulfilled in the Lord Jesus Christ in His resurrection. At the same time there is no record of anyone else who rose again after a sacrificial death thus fulfilling the features of the **Prajāpati-sacrifice.**

The Resurrection of Jesus Christ

The resurrection of the Lord Jesus Christ is a historical event. Since the first century, the central theme of Christian preaching has always been this truth. This was proclaimed by the Apostles of Jesus Christ very strongly. No historians ignored their proclamation or stated otherwise. In the Antiquities of the Jews Josephus, the famous Jewish historian of the first century, records as follows: "For He (Jesus) appeared to them on the third day alive again as the holy prophets had predicted."[101]

It has to be remembered that Josephus was not a Christian.

The resurrection of Jesus Christ is clearly recorded in the Holy Bible. From the Gospel of Matthew to the Book of Revelation - in the twenty seven books in the New Testament - we have very clear and accurate records about Jesus' resurrection. After investigating everything carefully from the beginning, St.Luke compiled an account of the things accomplished by Jesus and witnessed by the disciples. He narrated the events of the resurrection and His appearance to His disciples in the final chapter of the Gospel. And when he started to write The Acts of the Apostles he summarised those events in this way:

"In the first account I composed, Theophilus, I wrote about all that Jesus began to do and teach, until the day He was taken up.... To these He also presented Himself alive, after His suffering, by many convincing proofs, appearing to them over a period of forty days, and speaking of the things concerning the kingdom of God." (Acts 1: 1-3. NASB)

Jesus Himself proved that He was alive after His resurrection.

St. Paul wrote:

"For what I received I passed on to you as of first importance that Christ DIED for our sins according to the Scriptures, that He was BURIED, that He was RAISED on the third day according to the Scriptures, and APPEARED to Peter, and then to the Twelve. After that He APPEARED to more than five hundred of the brothers at the same time, most of whom are still living, though some have fallen asleep. Then He APPEARED to James, then to all the apostles, and last of all He APPEARED TO ME also as to one abnormally born." (1.Cor.15:3-8)

Let us examine the statement of Paul in the light of the Gospel.

(a) It is certain that Christ Lived in this World

This point needs no further explanation. Nobody can deny that Christ lived in this world. He is the centre point of history.

(b) It is certain that Christ died on the Cross

When Paul was witnessing to the crucifixion and the resurrection of Jesus he said to King Agrippa: "What I am saying is true and reasonable. The king is familiar with these things,. . . I am convinced that none of this has escaped his notice, **because it was not done in a corner.**" (Acts 26:25,26) Many were involved in the crucifixion and thousands were eyewitnesses. St. John was one of them and he testifies that the soldiers came and understood that Jesus was dead. He writes: "But when they came to Jesus and found that He was already dead, they did not break His legs. Instead, one of the soldiers pierced Jesus' side with a spear, causing a sudden flow of blood and water. **The man who saw it has given testimony, and his testimony is true.**" (John 19:33-35)

About this Michael Green writes in his book The Day Death Died:

"This is evidence of massive clotting of the blood in the main arteries and is exceptionally **strong medical proof of death.** It is all the more impressive because John could not possibly have realized its significance to a pathologist. The 'blood and water' from the spearthrust is proof positive that Jesus was already dead."[102]

(c) It is certain Jesus was buried

In accordance with Jewish burial customs Jesus was buried. A complete narration of the burial can be seen in the Gospel of John in its 19th chapter from verse 38 to 42. With Pilate's full knowledge and permission Joseph of Arimathea and Nicodemus took the body from the cross and buried it in the new tomb in the garden which was known to the Jews and the Roman authorities.

(d) It is certain that the tomb was properly sealed and guarded by the authorities

St. Matthew narrates this event as follows:

"The next day, one after Preparation Day, the chief priests and the Pharisees went to Pilate. 'Sir,' they said, 'we remember that while He was still alive that deceiver said, 'After three days I will rise again'. So give the order for the tomb to be made secure until the third day. Otherwise, His disciples may come and steal the body and tell the people that He has been raised from the dead...' 'Take a guard,' Pilate answered. 'Go, make the tomb as secure as you can.' So they went and made the tomb secure by putting a seal on the stone and posting the guard." (Matthew 27:62-66)

The guard did not consist merely of a couple of security guards. When we look carefully we can see the guard consisted of a group of soldiers.

(e) It is very clear that the tomb was empty on the third day

Even the enemies of Jesus could not deny that the tomb was empty. His friends and foes agreed together on that point. That was the reason why the chief priests told the soldiers (giving them a large sum of money), "You are to say, His disciples came during the night and stole Him away while we were asleep." (Matthew 28:13) The soldiers did as they were told. And St. Matthew recorded the understanding of the Jews as follows:'And this story (the story told by the chief priests and soldiers) has been widely circulated among the Jews to this very day." (verse 15) From this we can see that the Jews could not deny the truth of the empty tomb. They did not make any effort to regain the body. They did not charge any of the soldiers for negligence of duty. And it was quite impossible to believe that all the soldiers were sleeping at that particular time. Moreover, it was evident that they were anticipating this event -- at least a theft-attempt -- and that was the reason why they were guarding the tomb. The disciples of Jesus were scared to death and they were terribly afraid of the Jews and were hiding in their places. Nobody could believe these disciples would go to the tomb and steal the body of Jesus. So who opened the tomb? Who could roll away the stone and break its seal?

> From the Gospel of St. Matthew we read:
> "After the Sabbath, at dawn on the first day of the week, Mary Magdalene and the other Mary went to look at the tomb." (Matthew 28:1)

At the appearance of an angel shining like lightning the guards were so afraid that they became as dead men. (verses 3,4) "The angel said to the women,'Do not be afraid, for I know that you are looking for Jesus, who was crucified. He is not here; He has risen, just as He said. Come and see the place where He lay.' "(verses 5,6) They saw that the tomb was empty. The angel told them to tell the good news to all His disciples. "The guards went into the city and reported to the chief priests **everything that had happened.**" (verse 11)

The Appearance of Jesus

Jesus appeared to many people and gave them many convincing proofs that He was alive. Only some of the appearances were recorded in the Bible. Michael Green summarized these appearances as follows:

"He appeared to Mary Magdalene (Mark 16:9, John 20 1-18), to the women (Matthew 28:1-10), to Simon Peter (Luke 24:34; 1:Cor.15:5), to the disciples on the road to Emmaus (Luke 24:13-31), to the eleven and other disciples (Matthew 28:16-20; Luke 24:36-49; John 20:19-23; 21:1-14; Acts 1:3-9; 1.Corinthians 15:5-6), to Thomas (John 20:24-29), to James (1.Corinthians 15:7), to Joseph and

Matthias (Acts 1:22-23), to five hundred people at once (1.Corinthians 15:6), to Peter and John (John 21:15-24) and to Paul (Acts 9:4-6;1.Corinthians 9:1;15:8). Together, these appearances to individuals and to groups, to men and to women, in country and in town, in the upper room and by the open lake, constitute testimony to the resurrection that has to be taken very seriously indeed."[103]

When St. Paul wrote the fifteenth chapter of 1.Corinthians many of the eyewitnesses, among the five hundred brothers to whom Jesus appeared, were still living. Nobody questioned Paul when he wrote it for public reading.

Personal Testimonies of the Resurrection

St.Paul concludes the description of the appearances of Jesus with his personal testimony:

"....and last of all He appeared to me also, as to one abnormally born." (1.Cor.15:8).

Paul was not a Christian at that time but he was a well learned Jewish Rabbi and a zealous persecutor of Christianity. The book of Acts, chapter nine, describes how the Lord Jesus met him on the road to Damascus while he was killing the believers of Christ. The risen Lord Jesus Christ changed his life completely and he began to witness to the resurrection of Jesus. He dedicated the rest of his life to proclaim this glorious message to the learned and unlearned, to the Jews and the Gentiles, to ordinary men and to the officials in government. In the presence of high ranking officers and the leading men of the city, St. Paul gave this powerful testimony to king Agrippa:

"Why should any of you consider it incredible that God raises the dead? I too was convinced that I ought to do all that was possible to oppose the name of Jesus of Nazareth. And that is just what I did in Jerusalem. On the authority of the chief priests I put many of the saints in prison, and when they were put to death, I cast my vote against them. Many a time I went from one synagogue to another to have them punished, and I tried to force them to blaspheme. In my obsession against them I even went to foreign cities to persecute them. On one of these journeys I was going to Damascus with the authority and commission of the chief priests. About noon , O king, as I was on the road, I saw a light from heaven, brighter than the sun,blazing around me and my companions. We all fell to the ground and I heard a voice saying to me in Aramaic,

'Saul, Saul, why do you persecute me? It is hard for you to kick against the goads.'

Then I asked,

'Who are you Lord?'

'I am Jesus, whom you are persecuting', the Lord replied.

'Now get up and stand on your feet I have appeared to you to appoint you as a servant and as a witness of what you have seen of me and what I will show you. I will rescue you from your own people and from the Gentiles. I am sending you to them to open their eyes and turn them from darkness to light, and from the power of Satan to God, so that they may receive forgiveness of sins and a place among those who are sanctified by faith in me.' " (Acts 26:8-18)

Jesus transformed the lives of people like Paul. After the experience of transformation they began to proclaim the resurrection everywhere and nothing could stop them. In spite of punishments and further threats the disciples said to the officials: *"For we cannot help speaking about what we have seen and heard."* (Acts 4:20) As Michael Green states in his book, Man Alive, "Prison, torture and death could not alter their conviction that Jesus was alive." [104] Their sermons always centred on Christ's crucifixion and resurrection. Anybody can note that brave and outspoken tone of their sermons from the Book of Acts. As St. Chrysostom says,

"The courageous tone of their address itself is clear evidence of the truth of the resurrection".

The sacrificial victim of the Prajāpati-Sacrifice should return to life after the sacrifice! See how this truth is marvelously fulfilled in the resurrection of the Lord Jesus Christ.

Result #8

Identifying with the resurrection of Christ is the natural result of this aspect of the eternal sacrifice of God. St. Paul explains this truth through the symbol of baptism in this way:

"Or don't you know that all of us who were baptized into Christ Jesus were baptized into His death? We were therefore buried with Him through baptism into death in order that, just as Christ was raised

from the dead through the glory of the Father, we too may live a new life. If we have been united with Him like this in His death, we will certainly also be united with Him in His resurrection. For we know that our old self was crucified with Him... Now if we died with Christ, we believe that we will also live with Him." (Romans 6:3-8)

Thus we share the glory of the resurrection. We participate in the victory over sin and death. The new life in Christ is a victorious life.

The Answer to the Prayer of the Sages

"Mṛtyormā amṛtam gamaya"
(From death lead me to the eternal life).

The resurrection of Christ and its results are the answer to the prayer in the **Bṛhadaranyakopanisad.** Man is living under fear of so many things. The greatest fear of man is his death. He is totally helpless before the reality of death. Therefore, the wise sages prayed, "O Lord, from death lead me to the eternal life." Through the eternal sacrifice with all its characteristics and fulfillments, we overcome death, 'the last enemy' of mankind, and obtain immortality. About our bodily resurrection we have very clear teachings in the Holy Bible. In the first letter to Corinthians St. Paul devoted a full chapter to this subject. He writes, "Christ has indeed been raised from the dead, the firstfruits of those who have fallen asleep. For since death came through a man, the resurrection of the dead comes also through a man. For as in Adam all die, so in Christ all will be made alive." (1.Cor.15:20-22) He concludes: "When the perishable has been clothed with the imperishable, and the mortal with immortality, then the saying that is written will come true: 'Death has been swallowed up in victory.' 'Where, O death, is your victory? Where, O death, is your sting?' " (1.Cor.15:54,55)

The author of the book of Hebrews summarizes all these as follows:

"Since the children have flesh and blood, He (Jesus) too shared in their humanity so that by His death He might destroy him who holds the power of death - that is the devil - and free those who all their lives were held in slavery by their fear of death." (Hebrews 2:14,15)

The Testimony of People who Died With Christ

"To die is a gain" to St. Paul. Most of the believers in the first three centuries were severely treated and cruelly killed. But even at the time of their death they glorified God. Sorrows, fear or frustration could never diminish their joy of salvation and the assurance of eternal life. When St. Stephen was stoned to death he could see the glory of God. His last moment is recorded in the Acts of the Apostles:

"But Stephen, full of the Holy Spirit, looked up to heaven and saw the glory of God, and Jesus standing at the right hand of God. 'Look' he said, 'I see heaven open and the Son of Man standing at the right hand of God. . . While they were stoning him, Stephen prayed, 'Lord Jesus, receive my spirit.' Then he fell on his knees and cried out, 'Lord, do not hold this sin against them.' When he had said this he fell asleep." (Acts 7:55-60)

St. Stephen uttered these last words in the presence of many people who stoned him. Saul, the persecutor, was one among them. Thus we read from the Acts: "And Saul was there, giving approval to his death." The last words of Stephen might have worked in Saul's heart and that might be one of the reasons for the conversion of this ardent Jewish Rabbi.

Fleming H. Revell Company of New Jersey has published a book on the final moments and last words of famous people like D. L. Moody and Voltaire, entitled Voices From the Edge of Eternity. In this book John Myers has compiled testimonies of 250 people (including believers and non believers) who faced death.[105] Let me summarize the narration of the final moments of D. L. Moody from this book.

-- December 22, 1899. The famous revival preacher D. L. Moody flew away to the presence of God.

". . . Until within a few hours of the end, Mr. Moody shared with the family the conviction that he was improving. The day before, he had seemed rather more nervous than usual, but spoke cheerfully about himself. In reply to an inquiry if he was comfortable, he said:

"Oh, yes! God is very good to me -- and so is my family."...

"Life is very sweet to me, and there is no position of power or wealth that could tempt me from the throne God has given me."

"At three in the morning his son, W. R. Moody, came to his bedside. For several hours the patient was restless and unable to sleep but about 6 a.m. he quieted down and soon fell into a natural sleep.

He awoke in about an hour. His son suddenly heard him speaking in slow and measured words, 'Earth recedes-Heaven opens before me.'

His son's first impulse was to try to arouse him from what he thought was a dream.

'No, this is no dream, Will,' he said. 'It is beautiful! It is like a trance! If this is death, it is sweet! There is no valley here! God is calling me and I must go!'"

. . .

"Then it seemed as though he saw beyond the veil, for he exclaimed:

'This is my triumph: this is my coronation day! I have been looking forward to it for years.'

. . . .

'No pain! No valley!. . .If this is death, it's not bad at all. It's sweet!'

'This is my coronation day! It's glorious!' "

A.P. Fitt, the author of the biography of D. L. Moody, concludes the narration in this way:

"It was not like death, for he fell asleep quietly and peacefully."[106]

The Good News Weekly has reported the final moments of Pastor V. A. Thomas, a well known preacher in Kerala, India.

April 26, 1988 was his coronation day!

As the time approached, he said to his brothers and sisters in Christ:

"It's time. I have to go to my Father's house. Pray for me. Let me go."

"O Lord Jesus, Thy great love. . ." They all sang in Malayalam, their native language. After that, they started to pray. Finally, his wife also prayed.

Then he said in a soft voice:

"What a joy! What a peace! Let me go."

In the presence of many people he said these last words. At 11.00 p.m., on April 26, 1988, he flew away to the presence of the Lord Jesus Christ. [107]

The Testimony of the People who died Without Christ

At the same time the experiences of people who died without Christ are terrible and beyond description. The last hours of Voltaire, the noted infidel and French revolutionist, are also recorded. From the Voice From the Edge of Eternity I quote:

"When Voltaire felt the stroke which he realized must terminate in death, he was overpowered with remorse. . . He cursed them (his followers) to their faces and, since his distress was increased by their presence, repeatedly and loudly exclaimed, 'Begone! It is you that have brought me to my present condition. Leave me , I say-begone! What a wretched glory is this which you have produced for me!' . . .

For two months he was tortured with such an agony as led him at times to gnash his teeth in impotent rage against God and man.. . . Then, he cried out, 'I must die - abandoned of God and men!' ...

As his end drew near his condition became so frightful that his infidel associates were afraid to approach his bedside. . . Even his nurse repeatedly said that for all the wealth of Europe she would never see another infidel die. It was a scene of horror that lies beyond all exaggeration.

Such is the well-attested end of this man who had a natural sovereignty of intellect, excellent education, great wealth and much earthly honour."[108]

Without Christ death is real death - eternal separation from the presence of God. *"There will be weeping and gnashing of teeth." (Matthew 25:30)*

The Lord Jesus Christ - The Victor Over Death

With Jesus Christ, the Saviour, death is not death but a gateway to enter into everlasting life. The person who claims to be able to lead us from the valley of death should, by all means, be one victorious over death. Our death died with the death of our Lord and we live for ever with Him. The power of death is completely destroyed by His resurrection. Jesus said, *"Because I live ,you also will live." (John 14:19)*

The Vedas and the Upaniṣads talk about the Resurrection, not Reincarnation

In a strict sense, we can't find a single verse in the Vedas to support the theory of re-incarnation. However, many verses in the Upaniṣads are wrongly interpreted to prove this theory. But if we start our studies from the clear passages about immortality in Vedic literature we can easily see that the Vedas support the idea of the resurrection of the body.

The main theme of the **Kaṭhopaniṣad** is a search for life after death. It clearly states who will "escape from the mouth of death."

(". . . mṛtumukhātpramucyate.")[109]

The author of the **Upaniṣad** came to the conclusion that after death there is immortality, not reincarnation. This state of immortality is called Mukti. Other names like **'Uddhāra'** (the act of raising, pulling out), **'Rakṣa'**(the act of protecting) etc. also belong to this state of everlasting life denoting its meaning and significance. Mukti is the ultimate result of the **Prajāpati's** sacrifice. This will be discussed later in Chapter 15.

Die Once and After Death, the Judgment

The Holy Bible also does not support the man-made theory of re-incarnation. Thus the Word of God says: **"**Just as man is destined to die once, and after that to face judgment, so Christ was sacrificed once to take away the sins of many people, and He will appear a second time, not to bear sin, but to bring salvation to those who are waiting for Him." (Hebrews 9:27,28) Every one of us has to die once and to face the judgment of God. God appointed the **Man Christ Jesus** as judge of the living and dead and He will judge every one of us according to the glorious message of salvation that we heard. (Acts 10:42, Romans 2:16) Jesus made this clear as follows:

"For God so loved the world that He gave His one and only Son, that whoever believes in Him shall not perish but have eternal life. For God did not send His Son into this world to condemn the world, but to save the world through Him. Whoever believes in Him is not condemned, but whoever does not believe stands condemned already because he has not believed in the name of God's one and only Son. This is the verdict: Light has come into the world, but men loved

darkness instead of light because their deeds were evil." (John 3:16-19)

God has ordained this Man Christ Jesus to judge every man with justice. He has given proof of this to all men by raising Him from the death. (Acts 17:31.)

Resurrection - In the Fourth Stage of Sacrifice

This is the most glorious period of the living sacrifice where we enjoy the results of sacrifice. We have already seen in this fourth stage that we offer the sacrifice of giving and sharing and praising God. In this fourth stage, the sacrifice is a perpetual sacrifice which is continuing throughout eternity. The Word of God gives much importance to the continuity of this sacrifice:

"Through Jesus, therefore, let us continually offer to God a sacrifice of praise." (Hebrews 13:15).

We start to offer the sacrifice of praise through Jesus from the time we believe in Him and it will be continued through eternity. In the same way the sacrifice of good works and the sacrifice of sharing also will be continued. **"With such sacrifices God is pleased."** (Hebrews 13:16) Initially the sacrifice is very painful but in this stage it is most joyful. This is the reaping period. Jesus' sacrifice did not end in His tomb. He rose again and the efficacy of the sacrifice is continuing. In the same manner our living sacrifice in the Lord will be continued throughout eternity. In fact, that is our reward and the ultimate aim of our life. As the Church Fathers stated, "the chief-end of man is this: to glorify God and enjoy Him forever."[110]

Chapter 13

CHARACTERISTIC #9
THE FLESH OF THE MAN

After the sacrifice of the Passover Lamb, the Israelites ate its meat without anything left over according to the instructions. (Exodus 12:10). "The meat of the sacrificial animal should be eaten by the participants of the sacrifice." This ordinance was also honored and accepted in Vedic sacrifices from the beginning. Even though we do not have any specific reference for this in the **Puruṣasūkta** there are numerous passages in the **Brāḥmaṇas** supporting this view. They say that the sacrifice becomes the food of the gods. In the **'Sathapathabrāḥmaṇa** we read:

"Prajāpati gave Himself up to them: thus the sacrifice became theirs, **and indeed the sacrifice is the food of the gods."**[111]

We have seen earlier who the gods are in the light of the Scriptures. They are born of **rta** or sacrifice. These gods are the children of God who are born again by the power of the eternal sacrifice of the **Puruṣa-Prajāpati.** About gods, H. Aguilar writes:

"Not only are the gods born of **ṛta**, but they grow and nourish themselves by means of **ṛta.**"[112]

"Eat the Flesh of the Son of Man."

To everyone's surprise, Jesus said,

"I tell you the truth, unless you eat the flesh of the Son of Man and drink His blood, you have no life in you. Whoever eats my flesh and

drinks my blood has eternal life, and I will raise him up at the last day. For my flesh is real food and my blood is real drink. Whoever eats my flesh and drinks my blood remains in me, and I in him." (John 6:53-56)

Even His own disciples could not understand the mystery of His teachings. St. John records it in this way: "On hearing it, many of His disciples said, 'This is a hard teaching. Who can accept it?'"(v.60). They could not comprehend that the Lord Jesus Christ was predicting His own sacrificial death; much less His reference to eating His flesh and drinking His blood. Not entirely dissimilar is the imagery of the **Prajāpati-Sacrifice** in which the flesh of the victim is eaten by the gods for whom the sacrifice was performed.

The Last Supper

At the time of His last supper, Jesus explained this to His disciples. St. Matthew writes,

"While they were eating, Jesus took bread, gave thanks and broke it and gave it to His disciples saying, 'Take and eat; this is my body.' Then He took the cup, gave thanks and offered it to them, saying, 'Drink from it, all of you. This is my blood of the covenant, which is poured out for many for the forgiveness of sins..'" (Matthew 26:26,27)

"Do This in Remembrance of Me"

Jesus told us to remember Him and His eternal sacrifice. In the 'Holy Communion Service' we remember His sacrifice and renew the everlasting covenant. St. Paul writes to the believers,

"I received from the Lord what I also passed on to you: The Lord Jesus, on the night He was betrayed, took bread, and when He had given thanks, He broke it and said, 'This is my body, which is broken for you; do this in remembrance of me.' In the same way, after supper He took the cup, saying, 'This cup is the new covenant in my blood; do this whenever you drink it, in remembrance of me.'" (1.Corinthians 11:23-25)

In the next verse St. Paul gives us the meaning of the Lord's Supper: "For whenever you eat this bread and drink this cup, you *proclaim the Lord's death until He comes." (v.26)* Therefore the celebration of the Holy Communion or the Lord's Supper is the proclamation of the Lord's death.

Result No. 9

The corresponding result of the 9th characteristic of the sacrifice of the **Puruṣa-Prajāpati** is the communion or the fellowship with God and the saints (the believers). St. Paul asks the believers in Corinth,

"Is not the cup of thanksgiving for which we give thanks a participation in the blood of Christ? And is not the bread that we break a participation in the body of Christ?" (1.Cor.10:16)

In the Holy Communion Service we are symbolically eating the flesh and drinking the blood of the Son of Man. In other words, we are completely identifying with the crucified and the resurrected Christ who is our Master and Lord. When we identify with Him we live with Him. Jesus Christ Himself explains the concept of eating His flesh in this way:

"The Spirit gives life; the flesh counts for nothing. The words I have spoken to you are spirit and they are life." (John 6:63)

What You Eat that You are!

The old saying is very true! We have already noticed from the Vedas the gods (the children of God) are born of **rta** (sacrifice) and continue to live and nourish themselves by means of **ṛta.** Sacrifice is the food of gods. Jesus said:

"So the one who feeds on me will live because of me. . . he who feeds on this bread will live for ever. (John 6: 57,58)

The meaning is very clear. Every second, Jesus wants us to remember the meaning of His sacrifice and understand the eternal covenant that He has made by His own precious blood. That is the one and the only way to hide in Him. Our old self is dead along with the sacrifice and the new personality which we inherited in Christ will grow day by day until it reaches its perfection in Christ. In Christ we live forever.

Communion and unity are the most important results when we share the 9th feature of the sacrifice. Here we remember Jesus Christ and when we remember Him our mind will be filled with His sacrificial love which surpasses all understanding. Believers' minds focus on one point in one person, the Lord Jesus Christ. There we forget all other diversities and glorify and exalt one Man who is the centre of our adoration. He is worthy to be worshipped because He was slain for us and thus we get the privilege to be called the children of God. By His grace alone we are born in the family of God. By His death He paid the penalty of our sins and thus we are redeemed by His blood and freed from the fear of death. When He died on the cross our death died and through His resurrection we live forever. Therefore all born again believers should join together and worship Him. For them there is the one and only Lord to follow and they have one and only goal to fulfill.

In the Lord, the saints stay together in unity. There is no division in the Lord.

In the fourth stage of the living sacrifice we are able to do all good works through our Lord Jesus Christ.

Chapter 14

CHARACTERISTIC #10
THE TOTAL GIVING IN SACRIFICE
AND
THE OUTSTANDING RESULT

The sacrifice of the **Puruṣa-Prajāpati** is treated in the **Puruṣasūkta** as an act of total giving. Verses 8 and 9 start with this special idea which is full of significance. Let us quote the 8th verse:

"Tasmādyajñātsarvahutaḥ

sambhṛtaṃ pṛṣadājyaṃ

paśuntāmścakre vāyavyā-

nāraṇyān grāmyāśca ye"

{From that sacrifice in which (Puruṣa) offered all that He had, all these originated: sprinkled ghee and all kinds of animals of the sky, forest and country.}

See the next verse also:

"Tasmādyajñātsarvahuta

ṛca sāmāni jajñire

chandāṃsi jajñire

tasmādyajustasmādajāyata."

{From that sacrifice in which (Puruṣa) offered all that He had, the Ṛg, Sāma, Yajur Vedas and the chandas (sacred writings) were originated.}

Here we have to note the special emphasis given to the nature of the sacrifice. In this sacrifice the Man offered everything that He had. We could see through the previous chapters that the sacrifice of Jesus was an act of total giving. He gave us everything that He had including His life. We will see later in this chapter more details about this subject. But before that we have to understand the result of the total giving according to the verses in the **Puruṣasūkta.**

The Sprinkled Ghee and all Animals

As we have seen in verse 8 in the **Puruṣasūkta,** sprinkled ghee, birds of the sky, and the animals of the forest and of the country, all originated as the result of the total sacrifice of the **Puruṣa**. What is so important in creating animals and sprinkled ghee? We may exclaim at this if we miss the point. What is the significance of the sprinkled ghee and animals in the context of sacrifice? They are all sacrificial victims in animal sacrifices. Therefore, we can say in the light of this verse, that animal sacrifices originated as a result of the sacrifice of the **Puruṣa** in heaven. In order to represent the original sacrifice in heaven which formed in the heart of God, the animal-sacrifices were given to be performed on earth until the original sacrifice - the perfect and eternal sacrifice of Jesus - came down from heaven.

Ṛg, Sāma, Yajur Vedas and Chandas

From the 9th verse we read that all the three important **Vedas** and **Chandas (other sacred writings)** originated as the result of the Man-sacrifice. (Please note that **Atharva Veda - the fourth Veda -** is omitted here). The proclamation of the Man-sacrifice as the way of redemption is the main theme of the Scriptures. God wants to communicate the message of salvation through the Man-sacrifice to all people of the world.

The reason for the Scriptures is the love of God in the Man-sacrifice. God gave Himself for us in the perfect and eternal sacrifice. This is the sum and substance of the Holy Scriptures. Because of the sacrifice, all the Scriptures originated.

The central theme of the Holy Bible, from the book of Genesis to the book of Revelation, is the act of God to save fallen man through the redemptive sacrifice of Jesus Christ. It was written about Him in the scroll of ancients. After His sacrificial death and the resurrection, the Lord Jesus Christ Himself appeared to His disciples and taught them saying,

"Everything must be fulfilled that is written about me in the Law of Moses, the Prophets and the Psalms." (Luke 24:44)

Through the Spirit of Christ Himself the ancient sages could write all about the sacrifice of **Puruṣa** as the way of salvation. St. Peter puts it this way:

"Concerning this salvation, the prophets who spoke of the grace that was to come to you, searched intently and with the greatest care, trying to find out the time and circumstances to which *the Spirit of Christ in them was pointing when He (Jesus) predicted the sufferings of Christ and the glories that would follow."* (1.Peter 1:10,11) This revelation is so precious that "even angels long to look into **these things"** (1.Peter 1:12), as St. Peter points out.

Jesus Christ Himself is the revealed Word of God. "In the beginning was the Word... the Word was God." (John 1:1) The **Word** came down to earth in flesh and blood. That **Word** is Jesus and He Himself is **the last Word.** Therefore, the main theme or the main character of the revealed Word of God is the **Man (Puruṣa) Christ Jesus** who was separated Himself from the creation of the world for the eternal sacrifice for the final salvation of mankind. Yes, the Word of God came to man on earth as the result of the **Man-sacrifice** in heaven.

Church of God - the Outstanding Result of the Man-Sacrifice

It may be a great surprise to discover that the mystery of the Church of God is presented in the **Puruṣasūkta** as the outstanding result of the **Man-sacrifice.** The Church is a mystery to everybody until it is revealed. God revealed this mystery to His apostles after the sacrifice of Jesus Christ on this earth. St. Paul writes about that revelation as follows:

"Surely you have heard about the administration of God's grace that was given to me for you, that is the mystery made known to me by revelation, as I have already written briefly. In reading this, then, you will be able to understand my insight into the mystery of *Christ, which was not made known to men in other generations as it has now been revealed by the Spirit to God's holy apostles and prophets. THIS MYSTERY IS THAT THROUGH THE GOSPEL THE GENTILES ARE HEIRS TOGETHER WITH ISRAEL, MEMBERS TOGETHER OF ONE BODY, AND SHARERS TOGETHER IN THE PROMISE OF CHRIST JESUS."* (Ephesians 3:2-6)

The gospel - good news of salvation - also was written beforehand from the time of the creation of the world, but was hidden for long ages and was revealed at the appointed time of the Almighty God, *"so that all nations might believe and obey Him"*.(Romans 16:26) Through that faith and obedience we are one body in Christ Jesus. Now we are members together in the body of Jesus Christ. This is the mystery. Even though God already revealed this mystery through His holy apostles, it will remain as a mystery until we have a personal revelation from the Lord. If we pray with a sincere heart of love, the Lord will give us the revelation. Let us look to the verses of the **Purusasukta** with a sincere love of God and prayer.

Verse 11:

"Yatpuruṣaṃ vyadadhuḥ

katidhā vyakalpayan

mukhaṃ kimasya kau bāhū

kā ūrū pādā ucyete."

(When they sacrificed Man, how should the parts of the Man be perceived? Who is His face? Who are His arms? In what names should His tights and feet be known?)

Verse 12 is the answer:

"Brāḥmaṇosya mukham-

āsīdbāhū rājanyaḥ kṛtaḥ

ūrū tadasya yadvaisyaḥ

padbhyāṃ śūdro ajāyata."

(The face of the Puruṣa is the Brāḥmaṇa; the Shatriyas are His arms. The Vaiśyas are His tights. The Śūdras are (born from) His feet.)

All of these people are born of the sacrifice of **Puruṣa** and they are born from Him. There are four types of people in the world according to the Vedas: the **Brāḥmaṇas,** the **Shatriyas,** the **Vaisyas,** and the **Śūdras.** All these four types of people are parts of the body of **Puruṣa.**

Who are These People?

The scholars usually interpret these two verses almost the same way. The **Brāḥmaṇas,** of course, come from the top because they are the face of the **Puruṣa.** Similarly, the **Shatriyas** are the second group, the **Vaiśys** the third and the **Śūdras** the last.

The Brahmins often quote this portion to enforce the caste system in India. They even came to the conclusion that it was God who ordained the caste system. Thus they made a verse in the name of God: **"Cāturvarṇyaṃ mayā sṛṣṭam!"** ("The four caste system was made by Me - God!")

But, if we examine the 12th verse carefully we could see that all groups are members together in the body of the **Puruṣa** and are equally important for the functioning of His body. They all are perfectly joined together in **Puruṣa.** We often fail to grasp the real meaning which is the unity of the people in the body of **Puruṣa.** Our forefathers were very anxious to establish their supremacy over one another out of their egotism and spiritual blindness. And because of that reason alone they failed to become parts of the body of **Puruṣa.** Another man would say: "I don't believe in all these things. Why should I become a part of somebody? I don't want that!" Surely he also will not be a part of **Puruṣa** because the Almighty God does not compel anybody to believe in His mystery.

Then, who are the members of the body of **Puruṣa?** The original verses in the **Puruṣasūkta** say that all these people are the direct result of the **Man-sacrifice** - these people are born from the sacrifice. We have seen many other objects that originated from the sacrifice but the creation of these people as different parts of **Puruṣa** is the most important and the outstanding result of the sacrifice.

Then, who are these people? Most assuredly we can say that those who willingly set themselves apart to share the sacrifice and believe in it with their full heart will be the members together in the body of **Puruṣa.** To Puruṣa, all parts of His body are equally important and precious. We have already seen them before in another name 'gods' (**devas**) or the children of God. They are born of **ṛta** (sacrifice) and grow and nourish themselves by means of **ṛta.**

Who Are These People in the Book of Revelation?

This revelation will be very clear when we come to the New Testament concept of the Church of God. In the book of Revelation St. John saw the vision of the great multitude in white robes from every nation, tribe, people and language, standing before the throne and in front of the Lamb crying out in a loud voice holding palm branches in their hands:

"Salvation belongs to our God, who sits on the throne, and to the Lamb.' " (Revelation 7:9,10)

The main theme of their song is Salvation through the Lamb of God who was slain by the creation of the world. In the vision the elders asked John,

"These in white robes - who are they, and where did they come from?" (verse 13)

John answered,

"Sir, You know."

The angel replied to him:

"These are they who have come out of the great tribulation; they have washed their robes and made them white in the blood of the Lamb." (verse 14)

Who are these people? They are the people from every nation, tribe and language of the planet earth. They had suffering on earth. But we see them enjoying everlasting joy of salvation in heaven. What was their qualification to obtain immortality?

"They have washed their robes and made them white in the blood of the Lamb."

These people are the direct result of the sacrifice of the Lamb of God. Even though they are coming from various nations and backgrounds, they all are wearing white robes which are washed by the blood of the Lamb of God. They unanimously sing one song. Their hearts unite together in worshipping their Lord and Saviour. They worshipped Him with one mind:

"Worthy is the Lamb, who was slain, to receive power and wealth and wisdom and strength and honour and glory and praise!" (Revelation 5:12)

He is worthy to be worshipped because He was slain in the sacrifice and with His blood He purchased people from every tribe, language and nation. (Revelation 5:9) The mystery that was revealed to St. Paul was this:

"Through the gospel the Gentiles are heirs together with Israel, members together of one body, and sharers together in the promise in Christ Jesus." (Ephesians 3:6)

It means that through the gospel - the good news of the sacrifice - all people of the world are invited to this glorious mystery of God. The Church is known as the body of Christ. (Eph.4:13) The believers are called the parts of His body as we see with the people in **Puruṣa**. St. Paul explains this concept more clearly in his letter to the believers of Corinth:

"The body is a unit, though it is made up of many parts; and though all its parts are many, they form one body. SO IT IS WITH CHRIST. For we were all baptized by one Spirit into one body- whether Jews or Greeks, slave or free- and we were all given the one Spirit to drink." (1.Cor. 12,13)

In the New Testament times various types of people - Jews and Greeks, slaves and free men - believed and became members of the body of Christ. But in Christ they are all one Spirit. Slaves and free men are equal in the body of Christ. Each member has his own position in the church or the body of Christ. St. Paul continues to describe this as follows:

"Now the body is not made up of one part but of many. If the foot should say,'Because I am not a hand, I do not belong to the body,' it would not for that reason cease to be part of the body. And if the ear should say, 'Because I am not an eye, I do not belong to the body,' it would not for that reason cease to be part of the body. If the whole body were an eye, where would the sense of hearing be? If the whole body were an ear, where would the sense of smell be? But in fact God has arranged the parts in the body, every one of them, just as He wanted them to be... As it is, there are many parts, but one body." (1.Cor.12:14-20).

The parts are important for one and only reason: they are united together in the body of **Puruṣa.** As long as the part - whether it is small or big - remains with the body, it will continue to function and be alive. *But if any member is removed from the body, the member will be lifeless.* St. Paul exhorts every believer to be united to the body of Christ. In his letter to the Ephesians he writes*: "Make every effort to keep the unity of the Spirit through the bond of peace. There is one body and one Spirit-...* " (Ephesians 4:3,4) It was God who placed us in His body to produce the fruit of sacrifice and to live a life of love in harmony. "From Him (Jesus) the whole body, joined and held together by every supporting ligament, grows and builds itself up in love, as each part does its work."(Eph.4:16) When each member stays with the body of Christ the blood of Jesus circulates throughout the parts of the body and that blood circulation which we need every second will keep us alive in Christ. This is a profound mystery.

Divisions and Fighting In the Churches - Why?

Today, we can see fighting and divisions in the churches. Very often we hear about church splits and politics among the so-called believers! The only reason we can find is this:

They forget Christ and remember many other things. We see fighting for position and fighting for doctrines. They forget Christ **the whole Man**. Jesus said to us: *"Remember me." The man who remembers Jesus will forget all other things.*

The person who knows Jesus's sacrificial love will be willing to sacrifice anything for the Lord. Whenever problems arose in the early church, St.Paul encountered the situation by reminding them of Jesus. When he discovered a division in the Corinthian church he immediately wrote to them:

"Is Christ divided? Was Paul crucified for you?" (1.Cor.1:13) Paul was telling them to remember Jesus who had been crucified for them. Jesus says, "Whoever has my ommands and obeys them, he is the one who loves me." (John 14:21). "My command is this: Love each other as I have loved you. Greater love has no one than this, that he lay down his life for his friends." (John 15:12,13) St. Paul exhorts us: "Live a life of love, just as Christ loved us and gave Himself for us as a **fragrant offering and sacrifice to God."** (Ephesians 5:1) Jesus says,*"By this all men will know that you are my disciples, if you love one another."* (John 13:35) Therefore true believers will be visible by their fruits. In fact, the assembly of the true believers is called the **Church.** God will always approve them. St. Paul wrote to the Corinthian Church: "No doubt there have to be differences among you to show which of you have God's approval." (1.Corinthians 11:19)

Actually, there is no division in the real Church of God. Since the Church is the body of Christ, it cannot be split. St.Paul wrote:

"The eye cannot say to the hand, 'I don't need you!' And the head cannot say to the feet, 'I don't need you!'. . . But God has combined the members of the body and has given greater honour to the parts that lacked it, so that there should be no division in the body, but that its parts should have equal concern for each other." (1.Cor.12:21-25)

Those members who are united with the Lord Jesus Christ, the Head, cannot be divided at all. The parts of the body without the head will be lifeless, separated and scattered.

Jesus Gives All to His Church

The relationship of Christ and the Church is further illustrated by the comparison of the relationship of husband and wife.

St. Paul writes:
"For the husband is the head of the wife as Christ is the head of the Church, his body, of which He is the Saviour." (Eph.5:23)

Therefore as the true and faithful wife submits to her husband in everything the Church should submit to her Lord Jesus Christ.

"Christ loved the Church and gave Himself up to her to make her holy." (Ephesians 5:25,26)

Whatever He has He gave to His church. Through His sinless and perfect sacrifice Jesus makes His Church sinless and perfect. He shares His cross with us, His Church, to bring us to His glory. We share everything that He owns. "We are heirs of God and co-heirs with Christ, if indeed we share in His sufferings in order that we may also share in His glory." (Romans 8:17) With Jesus we share His eternal victory over sin, disease and death. With Jesus we are going to live for ever and ever. Whoever believes in Him will live with Him eternally. Jesus said to His disciples: "I will come back and take you to be with me that you also may be where I am." (John 14:3) We who believe in Him will live with Him everlastingly. Through the great gift of revelation St. Paul says:

"The two will become one flesh. This is a profound mystery- but I am talking about Christ and the Church." (Eph.5:31,32)

Thus in this mystical union with Christ we, the Church, live in Him forever. Jesus says, **"Because I live, you also will live."** (John 14:19) That is the ultimate result of the **Man-sacrifice.** He gave us Himself and everything that He owns. Surely it was a total giving as we have seen in the **Puruṣasūkta.**

The Testimony of St. Paul

Understanding this great love, St. Paul sacrificed everything at the feet of Jesus. When he was called to serve the Lord he served Him as a slave serves his master. He called himself a **"prisoner for the Lord."** (Ephesians 4:1) He was captured by the sacrificial love of Jesus Christ. He boldly proclaimed: **"For me, to live is Christ and to die is a gain."** (Philippians 1:21) He offered His body as a living sacrifice and lived a life of love as he has exhorted all believers to do. God made his martyrdom known to him and thus he knew beforehand that he was going to be identified with the sacrifice of Jesus by his death. He wrote to Timothy:

"For I am already being poured out like a drink offering, and the time has come for my departure. I have fought the good fight, I have finished the race, I have kept the faith. Now there is in store for me the crown of righteousness, which the Lord, the righteous judge, will award to me on that day. . ." (2.Timothy 4:6-8)

Soon after that he was beheaded by the Roman Emperor and thus he gave his life completely in the love service of the Lord Jesus Christ. Still the powerful and challenging voice echoes in the world:

"For I am convinced that neither death nor life, neither angels nor demons,. . .will be able to separate us from the love of God that is in Christ Jesus our Lord." (Romans 8:38,39) St. Paul was sharing the sacrifice of Jesus. Concerning sharing the sacrifice Rev. Robert J. Daly quotes the opinion of Origen, an early church father, as follows: "Origen is also deeply concerned to show how Christians share in the sacrifice of Christ. This takes place first and foremost by martyrdom. For in this self-immolation the Christian unites himself in the closest way possible with the sacrifice of Christ, sharing and even contributing to the vicarious benefit this sacrifice brings to others."[113]

The Author's Testimony and Prayer

My Lord Jesus Christ emptied Himself and gave me Himself and all that He possesses. Therefore, this is my humble prayer that I may love Jesus with all my heart, with all my strength and with all my soul. I submit myself to Christ in everything. Let me live a life of love and offer up living sacrifices daily. He gave us everything that He has. I pray, O Lord help me to follow your footsteps in sacrifice. Let me pour out my life as an acceptable and wise sacrifice to the Lord. Help me to live in the fourth stage of the sacrifice bearing the fruit of sacrifice.

We have been discussing a few important characteristics of the **Prajāpati-Sacrifice** in **Vedic** literature and the Holy Bible. We see that every one of them is completely fulfilled in the Lord Jesus Christ. The results of the sacrifice make the sacrifice the highest and most meaningful. Along with the Sages we can also say:

"Ṛta (sacrifice) is the highest (form of worship); no one goes beyond ṛta." [114]

PART III

MUKTI - THE ULTIMATE RESULT OF SACRIFICE

Part III

According to the Hindu religious texts, **Mukti** means the state of final salvation and that is the ultimate goal of every human being. The word **Mukti** originates from the Sanskrit root **muc** meaning 'to liberate, release, free and to deliver.' From this same root the word **Mokṣa** originated. Swami Nikhilananda says that the realization of **Mokṣa** is the chief end of man. To him **Mokṣa** means immortality.[115] The **Vedas** and the **Upaniṣads** bring us to the following conclusion: man reaches this final state of salvation or immortality through the perfect and eternal sacrifice of **Puruṣa.** From the **Puruṣasūkta** we have already noticed this earlier in the first chapter. The sixteenth verse of the **Puruṣasūkta** ends this way emphasising this point as follows: "**Through this (sacrifice) the sages obtain heaven."** According to the Vedas, attaining this state of immortality is the supreme goal of human life and therefore they named this way **Parāgati** (supreme way). In this third part we study about the supreme way from Vedic literature and the Holy Bible.

Chapter 15

THE WAY OF MUKTI IN THE KAṬHOPANIṢAD

In the **Kaṭhopaniṣad, mukti** is defined as escape from the mouth of death. That is the stage of deathlessness, which means everlasting life. We can find a sincere search for life after death in the **Kaṭhopaniṣad.** Death is the biggest enemy of mankind. How does a man escape from the mouth of death? The **Kaṭhopaniṣad** answers this question little by little through several verses in a very dramatic way. It is very interesting and exciting if we carefully follow the description of the text.

The Story of Naciketa and Death

The **Upaniṣad** starts with a story which beautifully illustrates the reality of death and the importance of eternal life.

The story goes like this:

A man named **Vajasravasa** sacrificed everything but his son, desiring peace of mind and blessing of the Lord. At this point his son **Naciketa** asked the father:

"To whom shall you give me?"

When the boy repeated this question two or three times the father became angry and told him:

"I will give you to **Yama,** the lord of Death."[116]

Hearing this the boy willingly went to the world of death. But **Yama,** the lord of Death was absent there for three days and three nights. **Naciketa** patiently waited for him without food or drink. After three days Death encountered him and said:

"I am very sorry for my absence. I appreciate your patience. So

I would like to give you three boons in order to compensate for my absence of three days and three nights."

As the first of those boons **Naciketa** asked that his father be not anxious about him, and have peace.

"So let it be", Death said, "Your father will see you alive and continue to love you and he shall sleep in peace."

As the second boon **Naciketa** said: "O Death, there is no fear in heaven. You, Death, will not be there. . . There will not be any hunger or thirst. Sorrow will be no more. Heaven is filled with joy and happiness. O Death, you know the fire sacrifice that leads to heaven. Teach me that sacrifice. This is my second boon."[117]

Yama gave him this boon also. He explained the fire-sacrifice and called that sacrifice after his name - **Naciketa-sacrifice** in memory of him.

The Question About the Life After Death

The third boon that **Naciketa** asked was touching the heart of immortality:

" O Death, still I have this doubt - some say when a man dies 'he exists' and some say 'he does not'. I should know this. Explain it to me."[118]

But Death was not willing to give this boon to **Naciketa.** He told **Naciketa** to ask something else.

"No boon can be equal to this boon. I want to know what happens to man after his death" Naciketa insisted.

"Ask for sons and grandsons who will live a hundred years, for elephants, horses, gold and herds of cattle, a vast territory on earth. ."

When **Yama** was ready to offer all these great gifts **Naciketa** said,

"No boon is equal to knowing about eternal life."

The lord of Death urged him to ask for other wonderful things such as chariots, music, dance etc. But **Naciketa** was wise enough to say,

"All these things, O Death, are not everlasting. The whole span of man's life on this earth is short indeed. So keep your chariots, horses, elephants, music, dances and merry making things with you. I want to know about immortality."[119].

Death was willing to give him anything but the knowledge of immortality. In fact, Death is the enemy of immortality. There is neither fear nor death in heaven. (**Svargeloke na bhayaṃ kincināsti na tatra tvaṃ. . .**)[120] When one enters into eternal life death is no longer there. This great truth of life is marvelously presented in this beautiful story of the **Kaṭhopaniṣad.**

Face To Face With Death

Death is not an imaginary character of a man-made fairy tale. It is real to every one of us. The question about life after death is always puzzling to mankind. Just like **Naciketa,** we also are very curious to know what will happen to us after death. Some people do not try to think about death saying that it is not a pleasant thought. No matter whether it is pleasant or unpleasant, everybody has to face it. No one can run away from this reality. However, in this century people are seriously thinking about the life after death. Many books have been published on the subject in the last two decades by eminent scholars and many of the books are still best sellers. As one author writes, "There is a new interest and openness today about the world's most fearsome mystery -- where we go after we die."[121] Dr.Maurice Rawlings' Beyond Death's Door and Joham Christoph Hampe's To Die Is Gain are two of the modern books about the life after death. Dr. Raymond Modi's books about the subject also are widely influential among the people all over the world.

Prepare Well for Immortality

Dr. Rawlings has a separate chapter in his book, Beyond Death's Door, on dealing with the dying. As a medical doctor his opinion has considerable weight. He writes,

> "When a patient asks me about his chances of surviving a serious illness,. . . I find it much more helpful to tell the patient truthfully that he has a serious disease (which I am frank to call by name) which could kill him; that he *should prepare himself in case it is fatal, and that he should have things settled with God so that either way he can't lose."*[122]

Actually, the time of preparation for eternity is when we live in perfect health. Since death is vital, every one of us has to know how to face death and enter into eternity peacefully. If you plan to study in a university, you will collect all the information about the institution before you enter there. A doctor will practice in a hospital only after he learns medicine systematically for many years. We are sure that we have to pass from this world into eternity. Therefore, we have to prepare ourselves for it. Death is an uninvited and surprising guest and it may appear at any time before us. Therefore, wise men are always prepared for it. Today is the preparation day. Each time when we attend a funeral service, or when we hear the news about the death of our loved ones, we feel sorry for them and try to comfort ourselves: "Death is real but I'm not going to die now or soon." But remember, when you die you can't think of it. Some people will die within a minute without even getting a warning of their death. A heart attack! A car accident! A plane crash! However, some people are fortunate enough to get some time before death to prepare for their eternity, although they might go through bodily and mental pain.

When the doctors say, "slight chance", most often the dying patient's response will be as follows: "No! I won't die soon. How can I die now! I have so many plans about the future." The doctors and psychiatrists will call this period, **"Denial". "Anger"** is usually the following stage; but it is of no use. The third stage is **"Bargaining".** In this stage the patient will turn to God or doctors for a possibility of life extension. When the patient knows that he is going to die he will enter into a fourth stage which is called,**"Depression".** The fifth stage is **"Acceptance".** Finally everybody has to accept the reality of death willingly or unwillingly. It is very hard to prepare himself for a peaceful death at this time. However, it is not too late and it is not totally impossible. But if he had already prepared for a life after death, his departure from this world would not be a tragedy.

Everyone of us has to learn how to die peacefully. Once an atheist's daughter was on her death bed suffering from all kinds of horrible visions. She told her father, "Father, you have taught me how to live luxuriously and how to make money. You sent me to the well-known universities where I studied literature, politics and science but I did not learn how to die peacefully. Father, teach me how to face this horrible death. . . " The father could not say anything to help her forget about death. He could not help the dying patient.

What is more important than life? God is the author of life and it is given to us, all living beings, by the creative power of God. As Sadhu Sunder Singh writes, "This life may change but it can never be destroyed, . . . this never means that death finally ends life."[123]

Heaven and Hell in the Vedas

From ancient times truth seekers have had visions about heaven and hell. Many are the descriptions of heaven in the **Vedas.**

According to the **Ṛg Veda:**

"Heaven is a place where light is perpetual. It is a beautiful place where there is happiness, pleasures, joy and enlightenment." [124]

We have already seen earlier from the **Kaṭhopaniṣad** that there will not be fear or death in heaven. The state of deathlessness is immortality. Therefore the most wonderful gift of God in heaven is immortality or everlasting life.

Similarly **Ṛg Veda** refers to hell, the place of eternal death and eternal punishment. *Here, hell is referred to as a deep pit, and a place of darkness, where the wicked fall down headlong.*[125] Jesus Christ also taught us about heaven and hell very clearly more than anyone else. Everybody has to continue his or her life in heaven or in hell eternally.

Therefore, as the church fathers and the sages say, the chief end of man is enjoying God forever in heaven in a state of deathlessness or **Mukti.** How blessed is the man who has the assurance of eternal life in heaven with God Almighty! The sages who prayed, **"Mṛtyormā amṛtam gamaya" (From death lead me to immortality),** definitely sought everlasting life and they got the answer. The answer was not invented by the Vedic sages but it was given to them. They presented the way of salvation to the truth-seeking people through the **Upaniṣads.**

The Teachings of Eternal Life in the Kaṭhopaniṣad

In the first part of the **Kaṭhopaniṣad,** the author has aroused the desire in the hearts of spiritual aspirants to know the hidden truths about death and life hereafter. He then goes on to reveal by and by divine knowledge as to the way to attain immortality or final salvation. **The Upaniṣad** demands our full attention in order to understand the way of salvation.

Uttiṣtata Jāgrata (Arise! Keep Awake!)

First of all, we have to seek the way of salvation sincerely and diligently. The **Upaniṣad** says:

"Uttiṣtata jāgrata prāpya

varānnibodhata

kṣurasya dhārā niśitā duratyayā

durgam pathastatkavayo vadanti."

{Arise! keep awake! Having obtained grace (varan=boons) learn (from God). The sages say that the path (of Mukti) is difficult to tread, and that the crossing over is as difficult as the sharp edge of a razor.}[126]

It is very hard to pass along the sharp edge of a razor. For man, it is impossible to travel this way by himself. However the writer does not want to discourage anybody from traveling along this path and he does not say it is totally impossible forever. But he tries to exhort the truth-seeker to be vigilant, to be awake and to give up all laziness. Like a watchman keeps awake in the battle field, he has to stay alert. That is the implied meaning of the word **Jāgrata.** A sleeper cannot travel this way and he will not know **Puruṣa,** man's only means of salvation. We can also hear a wake up call in the New Testament :*"Wake up O sleeper, rise from the dead, and Christ will shine on you."* (Ephesians 5:14)

Obtain God's Grace

Receiving grace from God is the next step for salvation according to the verse. If any one vigilantly seeks the way of salvation God will definitely pour His amazing grace upon him. The verse guides every seeker in obtaining grace and learning the way of salvation from Almighty God. (**prāpya varānnibodhata = having obtained varan -boons-, learn**). The word **varan** literally means boons. However, here the most important boon the heaven-seeker wants is the grace of God. This truth is revealed in another verse in the

Kaṭhopaniṣad as follows:

> **"Nāyamātma pravacanena labhyo**
>
> **na medhayā na bahunā śṛtena**
>
> **yamevaiṣa vṛṇute tena labhyastasyaiṣa**
>
> **ātmā vivṛṇute tanuṃ svām."**

[This **ātma** (Spirit of God or **Puruṣa**) is not obtained by many explanations, nor by the intellect, nor by much learning. God shows His mercy to whom He is pleased. To him God reveals Himself.)[127]

The Holy Bible explains the same idea:

"What then shall we say? Is God unjust? Not at all! For He says to Moses, 'I will have mercy on whom I have mercy, and I will have compassion on whom I have compassion.' It does not, therefore, depend on man's desire or effort, but on God's mercy." (Romans 9:14-16)

Salvation or immortality of man is completely dependant on God's mercy. The Word of God further emphasizes this fact: *"For it is by grace you have been saved, through faith - and this not from yourselves, it is the gift of God - not by works, so that no one can boast." (Ephesians 2:8,9)* As we have seen above, obtaining salvation is impossible for man by himself. Where man became helpless, God showed His mercy to redeem him from the deep pit of sin. But man has to humble himself and admit his real, pathetic condition before God. He has to confess his sins before God and ask for forgiveness. Then God will pour His mercy upon him. For it is written, *"God opposes the proud but gives grace to the humble." (1.Peter 5:5)*

Learn the Way of Salvation From God (Nibodhata)

When man humbles himself and seeks God with a sincere attitude he begins to learn from God. In that stage, God reveals Himself to the genuine seeker. When he knows the eternal God Almighty, he will taste death no more. In the **Kaṭhopaniṣad** chapter 3 verse 15 says that he will escape from the mouth of death. The full verse is given below:

"Aśabdamasparśamarupamavyaṃ

tathā-arasaṃ nityamagandhavacca yat

anādyanandaṃ mahataḥ paraṃ dhṛvaṃ

nicāyya tanmṛtyumukhātpramucyate."

{The man who knows God who is **aśabda** (not known or perceived by human sound), who is **asparśa** (not known by touch of the human hand), who is **arūpam** (formless, therefore not perceived by the eyes), who is **avyayaṃ** (unchangeable) who is **arasaṃ** (cannot be tasted by the human tongue), who is **nityaṃ** (eternal), who is **agandavat** (cannot be known by smell), who is **anādyanantam** (without beginning or end) and who is beyond all excellency, will definitely escape from the mouth of death}.

The verse suggests that it is impossible to know the Almighty God with our five senses such as the sense of hearing, the sense of touch, the sense of sight, sense of taste and the sense of smell. But at the same time, it is very important to know Him this way for attaining immortality.

The City of Eleven Gates

Another verse specifically says that for **Mukti** we have to know God with all our senses of the body and with our inner sense:

"Puramekādaśadvāramajasyāvakra cetasaḥ

anuṣṭāya na śocati vimuktaśca vimucyate. etadvai tat."

{He who knows God with his eleven gates (openings of the body and soul) and follows God, who is from the beginning without birth (**ajasya**) and who is of a sinless heart (**avakra-cetasah**), does not grieve (**na śocati**), is saved already (**vimukta**), and he will be saved in the future also. (**ca vimucyate**). This is verily that.}[128]

The usage '**puramekadaśadvāraṃ**' literally means the city

with eleven gates. But here, the city is the body of man. The interpretation of this passage from the Sacred Books of the Hindus is given below:

"The two openings of the eyes, the two ears, the two nostrils, and the mouth make up the seven upper orifices. The navel and the two lower make up ten. The eleventh is **brahmarandhra** in the skull." [129]

The eleventh opening in the skull is an imaginary one but it represents the inner eye that is the sense of the soul. The verse says that the man who knows God with all these senses is already saved even while he is living in the body. The verse continues to say that he will be saved. It is about his future and final state of his salvation. It means his future salvation is also completely secured if he knows **Puruṣa** with all his physical and spiritual senses and follows Him.

But how do we know God with our senses? We have already noted that no one can know God through his five senses. By the ear alone man cannot know God because the ear has its own limitations and God cannot be known by human sound. Nor are human words adequate to present God. We cannot see Him because He is formless **(arūpam).** That is the reason why God forbids the making of any image in the name of God. Thus God reminds His people, *"You saw no form of any kind the day the Lord spoke to you at Horeb out of fire. Therefore watch yourselves very carefully, so that you do not become corrupt and make for yourselves an idol, an image of any shape, whether formed like a man or a woman, or like any animal . ..* (Deut.4:15,16)

"No one has ever seen God," (John 1:18) the New Testament says. But in the same verse the Bible reveals the mystery: *"But God the One and the Only, who is at the Father's side, has made Him known."* Here, God has to open our inner eye of the soul (**brahmarandhra**) just like the Lord opened the heart of Lydia to hear the message of salvation in the Book of Acts. (Acts 16: 14) Jesus the Son of God who came down from heaven is the One and the Only Man **(Puruṣa)** who knows God and therefore He manifested Almighty God on earth to truth seeking people. Where man was unable to see God, God took the initiative to come down from heaven and take the form of a human being so that in Him we could see the glory of God. We have already studied the nature of the incarnation of God in Christ in the first two chapters. Even though He is the exact representation of the Almighty God Himself he has limited Himself to the Man of the 'ten fingers' (**daśāngulam**), as the **Puruṣasūkta** sings about Him. Jesus has revealed God on earth and we could see the glory of God in Jesus. Now according to the verses in the **Upaniṣad** man could see Him with his eyes, he could hear Him with his ear, he could touch Him, he could smell Him and he could taste Him. Now we can say with the *Upaniṣad that having known Him with all the senses of the body and spirit one escaped from the mouth of death.* **("...mṛtyu mukhāt pramucyate.")**

Revealing this St. John writes:

"That which was from the beginning, which we have heard, which we have seen with our eyes, which we have looked at and our hands have touched - this we proclaim concerning the Word of life. The life appeared; we have seen it and testify to it, and we proclaim to you the eternal life, which was with the Father and has appeared to us. We proclaim to you what we have seen and heard ,so that you also may have fellowship with us." (1. John 1: 1-3)

The author of eternal life or immortality (the escape from the mouth of death) is the eternal God Himself. When Jesus the Son of God appeared on this earth John wrote, **"The life appeared."** (verse 2) St. John knew Jesus Christ, experiencing Him by his physical and spiritual senses as he has written above. Therefore, knowing God the Almighty through the Lord Jesus Christ, the **Puruṣa,** is eternal life. In His prayer on behalf of the disciples to His Father, Jesus said:

"Now this is eternal life: that they may KNOW You, the only true God, and Jesus Christ, whom You have sent." (John 17: 3)

Chapter 16
PURUṢA THE SUPREME GOAL (PARĀGATI) TO KNOW HIM IS IMMORTALITY

We saw from the **Kaṭhopaniṣad** that knowing **Puruṣa** is the state of deathlessness or immortality. Chapter 3, verse 11 says there is nobody superior to **Puruṣa** and He is the end and the highest goal of mankind. The text also suggests how we may reach the supreme goal. Let us quote verses 10 and 11.

"Indriyebhyaḥ parā hyarthā

arthebhyaśca paraṃ manaḥ

manasastu parā buddhi

buddherātmā mahānparaḥ

mahataḥ paramavyakta-

mavyaktātpuruṣaḥ paraḥ

puruṣānna paraṃ kimcitsā

kāṣṭhā sā parāgati"

(The objects of the senses are superior to the senses. Mind is superior to the objects. Intellect is superior to the mind. Soul is superior to intellect. Unmanifested is superior to the soul. ***Puruṣa*** *is superior to the unmanifested. Nothing (nobody) is superior to* ***Puruṣa****. He is the chief end and the highest goal.)*

After we quote two more verses similar to this from the text (ch.6:7,8) we will explain the content of the verses.

"Indriyebhyaḥ paraṃ mano

manasaḥ satvamuttamaṃ

satvādadhi mahānātmā

mahato-avyaktamuttamaṃ

avyaktātu paraḥ puruṣo

vyāpako-alinga eva ca

yajñātvāmucyate jantu-

ramṛtatvaṃ ca gacchati"

(Mind is superior to the senses. Intellect is superior to mind. Soul is superior to the intellect. Unmanifested is superior to the soul. ***Puruṣa*** *is superior to the unmanifested. He is omnipresent.* ***One who knows Him becomes free and attains immortality.)***

The way to immortality is to know **Puruṣa.** But how can a seeker know Him and attain immortality? If we look carefully, we can see the writer explains the way step by step through the above quoted verses. Let us meditate on the verses carefully.

The Sense-Objects are Superior to the Senses (Indriyebhyaḥ Parāhyarthā)

Senses (**Indriyas**) means the five senses of man: ears, eyes, nostrils, skin and tongue. We have to know **Puruṣa** by the five senses for attaining immortality. Dr. D. M Datta, a great philosopher of India, writes in his book, The Six Ways of Knowing, "Of all the methods of knowledge, perception is by far the most important, for the obvious reason that it is the most fundamental."[130] The word perception is the translation of the Sanskrit word **pratyakṣa** which means present before the eyes or any other sense organ. Various states of experiences ascertained through these five senses are the sense-objects (**Indriyarthas**). We hear through the ears. Here, ears represent the sense of hearing and the experience of hearing is the sense-object. The ancient sage says in the **Upaniṣad** that the experience of hearing, the sense-object, is superior to the ears. Likewise the experience of touch is superior to the skin; vision is superior to the eyes; the smelling experience is superior to the nose and so is the taste to the tongue. If the experiences are not to be brought out by the respective sense organs they are quite useless and dead. Therefore the sage says the object of the senses is superior to the senses. In other words, we can say that the experience that is derived through the five senses is knowledge. Through experience you came to know **Puruṣa** and that is eternal life. According to the **Upaniṣadic** theory the experience of vision is greater than the eyes. If there can be vision without eyes there is no need of eyes. That means that without the help of our external eyes we can see **Puruṣa** and know Him and that vision is more important than our eyes. The taste - experience is greater than the tongue and we can taste and know **Puruṣa** even without our tongue. In the same way we can hear His voice without our ear. The **Upaniṣadic** sage says we can know **Puruṣa** through all other experience like touch and smell. This can be possible only when all other parts of man like mind, intellect, soul, etc. co-operate and work together for the growth of the total man. Let us further consider the **Upaniṣadic** view point in this subject.

Mind Is Superior to the Senses (Indriyebhyaḥ paraṃ mano)

The **Kaṭhopaniṣad** explains this in the third chapter verse 10, as well as in verse 7 in the sixth chapter. Chapter 3 verse 10 reads as **"Arthebhyśca paraṃ manaḥ" (the mind is superior to the sense objects)** whereas verse 7 in the sixth chapter starts as **"Indriyebhyaḥ paraṃ manaḥ" (beyond the sense is the mind)**. Both portions mean that mind is superior to the human sense organs and sense objects. Because mind is capable of comprehending and doing many things which the senses and sense objects can't, it is really superior to these. In order to reach the supreme goal of eternal life we have to know **Puruṣa** with our mind.

Let me quote another hymn from the text referring to the mind.

"Ātmānaṃ rathinam viddhi

'sarīraṃ rathameva ca

buddhim tu sārathiṃ viddhi

manaḥ pragrahameva ca"

(You know that the soul is seated in the chariot. The body is the chariot. The intellect is the charioteer. The mind is its reins.) [131]

In this verse the mind is the reins of the body. Explaining this the author of the **Upaniṣad** continues:

"Indriyāni hayanāhurviṣayāmsteṣu gocaran"

(Senses are called the horses and their sense objects are the roads.) [132]

A horse runs along the roads. The five senses of the human body run like a horse along the road of sense objects which are subjected to passion and pride. The nature of the horse is to run. In the same way the five senses have the natural tendency to gallop along the roads of worldly pleasures and sins. Therefore, the charioteer (intellect) has to control the horse (five senses) with the reins (mind). Otherwise the chariot (body) will be damaged. If the chariot is wrecked the soul that sits in the chariot will be dead.

Therefore it is very important for us to control our mind and look upon **Puruṣa**, the author of eternal salvation. We have to know Him with our five senses concentrating our mind upon Him. We read the Gospel of Jesus Christ and see Jesus, the **Puruṣa,** with our mind. We hear Him, touch Him and taste Him with our mind. When we meditate upon Him with our mind His presence and fragrance envelope us. Yes, we know Him with our mind. Quoting from the **Bṛhadāraṇyakopaniṣad** we can say that we actually see and hear with our mind.

"Anyatramanā abhūvam nādarsam,

anyatramanā abhūvam nāśrauṣamiti,

manasā hyeva paśyati, manasāśṛuṇoti

kāmaḥ sankalpo vicikitsā

'sraddhāśraddhā dhṛtiradhrtiḥ

hrīrdhīrbhīrityetatsarvaṃ mana eva..."

[My mind was elsewhere. (I was absent minded) (So) I did not see. My mind was elsewhere, therefore neither did I hear. By mind we see and by mind we also hear. Therefore desire, determination, doubt, belief and unbelief, courage and discouragement, shame, understanding, fear - all these are mind itself.] [133]

However, instead of concentrating my mind on **Puruṣa** I see my mind wanders here and there. The mind is wicked like a monkey that jumps too fast from one tree to the other. The mind goes to the destination point very fast before the body reaches there. The mind commits more sins than the body does. As it is written, **"the heart (mind) is deceitful above all things and beyond cure."** (Jeremiah 17:9) If this is the condition of the mind how do I know **Puruṣa** with my mind?

The verse in the **Kaṭhopaniṣad** gives us the answer.

Intellect Controls the Body and the Mind

"Manasastu parā buddhi" (Intellect is superior to the mind.) The verse in the **Kaṭhopaniṣad** quoted above continues in this way. We have just mentioned above that the intellect is the charioteer of the chariot which is the body. So this charioteer controls the horse of the chariot which is the five senses of the body. When the five senses are subjected to the intellect through the reins (mind) the body and mind will automatically turn to **Puruṣa** who is the supreme goal and the author of immortality.

Why does the intellect control them? It controls them because of the superiority of the intellect and that is the job assigned by God to the intellect or **buddhi.** Here, **buddhi** means the discriminating intellect given by God. By this we are reasoning and discriminating between good and bad. We determine to reject bad and accept good by this reasoning capacity. The mind will run through the areas of bad and good as we have mentioned above. But the intellect immediately jumps to the scene and controls the mind. That is why the sage says that the intellect is superior to the mind. The word **buddhi** can be interpreted as **conscience** when we understand the nature of the work of the intellect. The seventh verse of the sixth chapter has the same meaning: "**Manasaḥ satvamuttamaṃ**" which means mind is superior to **satvam (personality)**. This word **satvam** can also be translated into intellect yet the word has a much deeper significance. A person has to look toward to **Puruṣa** and know Him with all his mind, with all his intellect (conscience) and also with all his personality.

Soul Is Superior to the Intellect And Personality

With our soul we have to know **Puruṣa** for our salvation. Soul (**ātma**) is the one who lives in the body. He is the one who sits in the chariot. The charioteer and the reins and the horses - all are for the person who sits in the chariot and all of them are subjected to him. Therefore the **Upaniṣad** says that soul is superior to the intellect and personality. ("**Buddherātmā mahānpara**' - chapter 3 verse 10 - "**satvādadhimahānatmā**" - chapter 6 verse 7.) The soul will be happy inside when everything is going in order.

Rebellion In the Faculty of Man

However, very often we can see fighting in the faculty of man. When rebellion occurs everything will be in disorder. The horse (senses) will not be controlled by reins (mind). The mind rejects the orders of intellect or conscience. In this case the soul is helpless and is facing danger. Here, the whole faculty is suffering under the rebellion. Even though the mind is superior to the senses, the mind fails to subdue the senses according to the direction of the intellect. Even though the intellect has authority over mind, here it is incapable of using its power over the mind. Here we see that the man's intellect (conscience) is almost dead; it has lost its sensitivity. And automatically the soul enters the death process as it becomes sickly and continues to lose its vitality. Here the mind loses its king but still we see the mind will continue to work without the original king. But on close observation we can see a wicked king in the kingdom of the mind. The wicked king starts to lead the whole man to death which is quite the opposite of immortality. Who will lead the man from this situation and from death? Here, Intellect begins to cry to its superior Soul.

Incapability of Soul

But Soul cannot issue orders to its subordinates because the Soul is not capable of standing on its own. Soul is the most important person who sits inside the body of the chariot but at the time of rebellion Soul becomes powerless. If this situation continues without the interference of the one who has power over all the faculty of man the Soul will be dead eternally. In this situation the Soul and Intellect join together and look toward their Superior.

The Unmanifested is Superior to Soul

The two verses of the **Kaṭhopaniṣad** specify that the Unmanifested is superior to Soul. (**Mahataḥ paramavyaktaṃ; Mahato-avyaktamuttamaṃ.**)[134] The sage got the revelation of the unmanifested aspect of the faculty of the human being. It is obvious that this is one of the parts of the total man but it is not manifested until we know the most Superior **Puruṣa.** There will not be the unmanifested part in a human being until he properly knows **Puruṣa.** Therefore, we will come back to the portion after we understand the most superior position of **Puruṣa.**

Puruṣa is the Highest and the Supreme Goal

The above verses from the **Kaṭhopaniṣad** conclude with this powerful declaration:

"**Puruṣa** is superior to the unmanifested. Nothing (no one) is superior to **Puruṣa.** He is the highest and Supreme goal."

(avyaktat Puruṣah paraḥ Puruṣānna paraṃ kincit
sā kāṣtā sā parāgatih) (3: 11)

The same idea can be seen in the sixth chapter with a clear statement about eternal life:

". . . one who knows Him (the Supreme Puruṣa)
becomes free and obtains immortality."
(. . .yajñātvāmucyate janturamṛtatvaṃ ca gacchati.)
(verse 8)

Understanding his incapability, man cries with all his senses of the body, mind, intellect and soul to the most superior **Puruṣa.** Man has to understand the superiority of the **Puruṣa** who is the Man of eternal heaven. He has to know Him personally and he has to accept Him as his Lord and Master (**Guru**) and Saviour. In order to stop the rebellion in the faculty of man He will issue orders by His powerful word as soon as we invite Him to our aid. His word is creative. **Puruṣa** Himself is Word. When you start to follow this **Guru** the horses of the chariot (senses) will be submissive to the charioteer (Intellect). Here he can control the horse with its reins. The soul who travels inside the chariot will be very happy to sing:

> *"Praise the Lord, O my soul;*
> *all my inmost being, praise His holy name.*
> *Praise the Lord, O my soul,*
> *and forget not all His benefits-*
> *who forgives all your sins*
> *and heals all your diseases,*
> *who redeems your life from the pit.. . ."*
> (Psalm 103: 1-4)

To Know the Puruṣa is Eternal Life

The verse in the **Kaṭhopaniṣad** concludes with the concrete statement: **"One who knows Him (Puruṣa) becomes free and obtains immortality."** In fact, that is the main theme of the **Upaniṣad**. That is the answer to the perplexing question of mankind concerning the life after death, the greatest mystery in the world. About eternal life Jesus Christ also taught us the same truth. Let me quote once more the prayer of Jesus to His Father just a day before He gave Himself in sacrifice:

> *"Father, the time has come. Glorify Your Son, that Your Son may glorify You. For You granted Him authority over all people that He might give eternal life to all those you have given Him. Now this is eternal life: that they may KNOW You , the only true God, and Jesus Christ, whom You have sent."* (John 17:1-3)

Misunderstanding Puruṣa Leads People to Death

Knowing or understanding **Puruṣa** is eternal life. At the same time, misunderstanding **Puruṣa** is death and eternal separation from the living God.

When we go through the history of Indian philosophy we see a lot of discussions and studies about **Puruṣa.** This author can appreciate the great scholarship and hard work of the Eastern Philosophers. Dr. Jadunath Sinha, M.A. Ph.D., the Professor of Philosophy in Meerut College, has written A History of Indian Philosophy in two volumes. (Volume 1 contains 912 pages and Volume 2 contains 762 pages.)[135] From the first chapter of the second volume of his book we see the history of different interpretations of the word **Puruṣa** from the time of **Sāmkhya. Sāmkhya** school of Philosophy also teaches that **Puruṣa** is the subject of knowledge. Dr. Sinha writes in the light of **Sāmkhytattvārthakaumudi** about the eternal nature of **Puruṣa** as follows:

> **"All things change every moment except the Puruṣa."** [136]

But at the same time they teach that there are many **puruṣas.**

Dr. Sinha summarizes their view:

"The Sāmkhya recognizes the existence of many selves or **puruṣas** and puts forward arguments for their existence.

(1) Birth, death and the sense-organs are different in different persons. If there were one self (**puruṣa**) only, the birth of one person would lead to the birth of all; the death of one would lead to the death of all and the defects in sense-organs in one would lead to the same defects in the sense-organs in all. . .

(2) If there were one self (**puruṣa**) in different bodies, the activity of one person would lead to the activity of all. But, in fact, different persons are engaged in different kinds of activity. . .

(3) Different selves (**puruṣas**) are equipped with different moral endowments. . ."[137]

Puruṣa and Self

It is very clear that these philosophers totally misunderstand **Puruṣa** who is presented in the **Vedas** and **Upaniṣads**. They translate the word **Puruṣa** as 'self'. Many of the modern teachers of Hinduism follow the **Sāmkhya** philosophy and translate **Puruṣa** as 'self'. For example see the translations of the **Upaniṣads** by Swami Ranganathananda or Swami Prabhavananda. They use the word 'self' for **Puruṣa** in their works.[138] We cannot find this meaning for the word in the dictionary. V. S. Apte's Sanskrit English Dictionary gives the meaning of **Puruṣa** in this way: "**A male being, man**".[139] The same meaning is given for the word **Puruṣa** in the Dictionary of Sir Monier Monier-Williams also. Almost all the regional languages of India like Hindi and Malayalam borrowed the same term **Puruṣa** from Sanskrit and use it without any change of meaning. Then how did the scholars find the word 'self' for **Puruṣa?** In answer to the arguments of the **Sāmkhya** philosophers let me say: It is true there are many selves in this world. It is also true that there are many **puruṣas** (men) in this world. But we have to understand that the 'self' is different from **Puruṣa** in Vedic literature. When we read the description of **Puruṣa** from the **Vedas and the Upaniṣads** we immediately recognize that there is one and only one **Puruṣa** in this universe.

The Kaṭhopaniṣad is very clear in its proclamation that there is none superior to **Puruṣa.** And also it states that He is the Supreme goal. **(parāgati).** There cannot be two supreme persons in this world.

From the first chapter of this book we have already seen the majesty and uniqueness of the **Puruṣa** who has a thousand heads, a thousand eyes and a thousand feet. He is called **Parama Puruṣa** which signifies the one and the only supreme Man. We have already seen this supreme Man Jesus who came down from heaven. *"Puruṣa is all this universe, what has been and what will be."* This is the glory of Puruṣa according to the **Puruṣasūkta** that we have noticed. Understanding this, Jesus the Supreme Man said: *"I am the Alpha and the Omega who is and who was, and who is to come, the Almighty."* (Revelation 1:8) No man has made such a claim except Jesus. **Puruṣasūkta** glorifies Him as the Lord of immortality. There are **puruṣas** (men) in this world but none of them has this claim except the Supreme Man, the Lord Jesus Christ. He is risen from the dead and proved Himself that He is the **Puruṣa**, the Lord of immortality. **Puruṣa** is notable because of His Self-sacrifice. It was a total giving for us to inherit heaven. We have seen that it is also fulfilled in Christ Jesus. From the **Puruṣasūkta** we have noticed this Man should be a **Niṣkalanka Puruṣa.** There are ten characteristics like this in the **Puruṣa-Prajāpati's** sacrifice, completely fulfilled in the perfect Man Jesus. And the fact that knowing or understanding **Puruṣa** is eternal life was attested to by both the sages of the **Upaniṣads** and Jesus Christ Himself. Misunderstanding **Puruṣa** leads one to the path which is completely opposite to eternal life. That is the way to death.

The philosophers are mistaken in their assumption that there is a **Puruşa** in every human being as everybody has sense organs, mind and intellect. If everyone has **Puruşa,** the Master (**Guru**), as his Lord everybody should be saved. If this is true, there will be no need to write that one who knows **Puruṣa** will be saved. Since the heart of man is sinful, **Puruṣa,** the Almighty God, cannot dwell there. Understanding this reality man has to humble himself and seek the grace of God for salvation as we saw earlier from the **Kaţhopanişad**. To him God reveals his plan of salvation through the sacrifice of **Puruşa.** Here, man has the responsibility to receive Him with a full heart for salvation. God in His mercy and everlasting love communicates to the truth-seeker the glorious message of salvation through the eternal sacrifice of **Puruṣa.** However, only on the basis of repentance of his sin, acceptance of the message and his invitation to **Puruşa** does He come to the heart of a man. **Puruṣa** - the Spirit of God - enters in him to lead him from darkness to light, from unreal to the real and from death to eternal life. Here, the senses, mind, intellect and soul of the person - all are controlled by the Spirit of **Puruṣa.**

As it is written in the book of Romans, "The mind of sinful man is death, but the mind controlled by the Spirit is life and peace." (Romans 8:6) "You, however, are controlled not by the sinful nature but by the Spirit, if the Spirit of God lives in you. *And if anyone does not have the Spirit of Christ, he does not belong to Christ."* (Romans 8:9)

"But we have the mind of Christ" (1.Cor.2:16)

Chapter 17

KNOWING PURUṢA AS OUR GURU (MASTER)

In order to reach the state of deathlessness we have to know that **Puruṣa** is our **Guru** (Master). Eternal life is the gift of God and without **Puruṣa,** the Lord of immortality, we cannot receive it. In the same way the Vedas state that without **Guru** we will not reach the land of everlasting life. The qualifications of **Guru** and **Puruṣa** bring us to this important conclusion: **Puruṣa and Guru are one and the same person.**

Guru literally means master or teacher. In this modern society we have so many masters and teachers .People call them **Gurus.** But according to the definition and explanation of the word **Guru** from the **Upaniṣads** there is one and only one **Guru** in this universe.

Let me quote from the **Advayatārakopaniṣad**:

"Guśabdastvandhakārah syād

ruśabdastannirodhakaḥ

andhakāra nirodhitvād

gururityabhidhīyate"

(The sound 'gu' means darkness.'Ru' means its destroyer. He who destroys darkness is called Guru.) [140]

Another important text, **Gurugīta (The Hymn of Guru),** also gives us the same interpretation for **Guru** with some more details:

"Gu kāraścandhakārohi

ru kārasteja ucyate

ajñānagrāsakaṃ braḥma

gurureva na saṃśayaḥ."

{The sound 'gu' means darkness. 'Ru' is told as light. No doubt, Guru is God (Braḥma) who destroys the dark of ignorance.} [141]

Note the emphasis given here : **"No doubt, Guru is God Himself."** Only God can destroy darkness - sin - ignorance - of the world.

The **Upaniṣads** were not mistaken when they ascertained that **Guru** is God Himself. With utmost assurance the sages proclaimed:

"Gurureva param braḥma

gurureva parā gatih

gurureva parāvidya

gurureva parāyaṇam

gurureva parākāṣta

gurureva paraṃ dhanaṃ . . . "

{Guru Himself is Supreme God (para braḥma),
Guru Himself is the Supreme way (parāgati),
Guru Himself is the Supreme knowledge (parā vidya),
Guru Himself is the Supreme journey (parāyaṇam),
Guru Himself is the Supreme climax (parākāṣta),
Guru Himself is the Supreme wealth. (paraṃ dhanaṃ)} [142]

Beyond any doubt we can say that **Guru** is not an ordinary human being. He is God Himself. But this **Guru** is **the way** for the man of this earth for his journey. This way is not one of the good ways but this is the supreme way. Similarly this journey is not one among many good trips but it is the best and the supreme. The Sanskrit word **param** is used to convey this idea of superiority. In the same manner, He is not one of the good subjects of learning but He is the supreme knowledge. This is also for the common man of the world. This **Guru** offers the man of the earth the supreme way, the supreme knowledge, the supreme journey, the supreme wealth and every good thing in its state of climax because He is the supreme God from heaven. But in order to give these supreme gifts, God of heaven has to come down to the earth as a man. He has to live among the ordinary people as a man to teach them the supreme knowledge. Man on earth has his own limitations in learning the divine mysteries of God in heaven. In order to learn anything he has to see things in front of his eyes and hear words in his ear; he has to touch it; he has to smell it and he has to taste it. To be educated in the supreme knowledge, people of the world with their sinful nature are unable to go into heaven. That is the reason why God Himself came down as **Guru** to teach them the supreme way to heaven. Since He Himself is the way He has to be here among mankind. As we have seen in the **Aśvattha tree** (the inverted tree which came down from heaven) and in the Man-Sacrifice in the **Puruṣasūkta,** the concept of **Guru** in Vedic literature also communicates the message of the incarnation of God.

The Lord Jesus Christ - Our Guru

Let us consider now how all these important characteristics of **Guru** are completely visible in the Lord Jesus Christ who came down from heaven as the Son of Man (**Puruṣa**).

(1) Guru who Destroys the darkness of Sin

According to the **Upanisads, Guru** is the one who destroys darkness. He is the light. Darkness is the symbol for sin and death. When the sages prayed to be led from darkness to light they really meant that they might be led to the forgiveness of their sins. Their ultimate need was to obtain everlasting life. They conclude their prayer with this definite petition:

"Mṛtyormā amṛtam gamaya - From death lead me to immortality."

Therefore, to destroy darkness means to destroy sin and death. That was the mission of Jesus Christ. He destroyed the power of sin and death through His self-sacrifice on the cross. He is the light of the world. Jesus said:

"I am the light of the world. Whoever follows Me will never walk in darkness, but will have the light of life." (John 8:12)

Here, in the verse of Jesus, we see very clearly that the light is life. From there, we can understand Jesus' interpretation of darkness. He said that the light is life and therefore it is obvious that the word 'darkness' indicates death.

The **Bṛhadāraṇyakopaniṣad** interprets darkness and light in the same way:

"Tamasomā jyotir gamayeti, mṛtyurvai tamaḥ,
jyotiramṛtam..."

{In the verse 'from darkness lead me to light', darkness is death; light is life (amrtam).} [143]

Regarding Jesus the light of life, St. John writes:

"In Him was life, and that life was the light of men. The light shines in the darkness, but the darkness has not understood it." (John 1:5)

This light shines in darkness. Wherever this light reaches darkness runs away. As John writes about Him, this true light gives light to every man. (John 1:9) Some people receive the light but some reject it. Jesus Himself explains the reason for their rejection:

"Light has come into the world, but men loved darkness instead of light because their deeds were evil. Everyone who does evil hates the light, and will not come into the light for fear that his deeds will be exposed." (John 3:19,20)

Jesus also tells us who receive Him:

"But whoever lives by the truth comes into the light, so that it may be seen plainly that what he has done has been done through God." (John 3:21)

In accordance with the definition of the word **Guru** the Lord Jesus Christ is the destroyer of darkness. He is the light. As the sun penetrates the darkness so He penetrates the life of sinners. At the same time He was as pure as light; in Him there was no dark point. He annihilated the power of their sin and healed their sickness saying:

"Take courage, My son, your sins are forgiven." (Matthew 9:2) St. Matthew meaningfully quotes Jesus in this context:

"But in order that you may know that the Son of Man has authority on earth to forgive sins" - He said to the paralytic, "Rise , take up your bed and go home." (Matthew 9: 6)

Having been cleansed from his sin and the curse of disease he rose and went to his home.

Jesus, the Son of Man - **Puruṣa,** - has the authority to forgive sins because He has given His precious life as the eternal sacrifice of God. This is that sacrifice which was originally formed in the heart of God in heaven and later fulfilled in His crucifixion and resurrection with its full characteristics and significance.

(2) Guru Himself is the Supreme God (Gurureva paraṃ brahma)

The **Advayatārakopaniṣad** is very firm in its statement that the **Guru** Himself is the Supreme God. The so called **gurus** of the world do not have this claim. Even though there are many masters and teachers in this world, there is one and only one **Guru** in this whole universe.

That is the reason why the Lord Jesus Christ specifically taught us:

> **"But you are not to be called 'Rabbi' (Guru), for you have only one Master and you are all brothers. . . . Nor are you to be called 'teacher' for you have one Teacher (Guru) THE CHRIST."** (Matthew 23:8-10)

Jesus is God Himself who came down from heaven. Jesus gave this reply to Philip, one of His disciples who asked Him to show him the heavenly Father:

"Don't you know Me, Philip, even after I have been among you such a long time? Any one who has seen Me has seen the Father. How can you say, 'Show us the Father'? Don't you believe that I am in the Father, and the Father is in Me?" (John 14:9,10)

Jesus Christ is the radiance of God's glory and the exact representation of His being on this earth. "He is the image of the invisible God." (Colossians 1:15) "For in Christ all the fullness of the Deity lives in bodily form." (Colossians 2:9) That's the reason why the disciples could see in Christ "the glory of God as the only begotten of the Father, full of grace and truth." (John 1:14) We see the same thing in the **Gurugīta**:

"Gururādiranādiśca guruḥ paramadaivataṃ." (Guru is adi (beginning) and anadi (without beginning) and He is the Supreme God.[144]

(3) Guru Himself is the Supreme Way (Gurureva parāgati)

In this context, **gati** means way. In another place we have translated this word **'para gati'** as supreme goal. Goal is the end of the way. In order to achieve the goal we have to travel by the way. The Lord Jesus Christ said:

"I am the WAY and the truth and the life. No one comes to the Father except through Me." (John 14:6)

Jesus boldly made this statement because He knew the way. He is the one who came down from the Father in heaven. He said:

"No one has ever gone into heaven except the one who came from heaven- the Son of Man (Puruṣa).
(John 3:13)

We have studied earlier the teachings in the **Upaniṣads** that tell us that to know the **Puruṣa** is the way to the land of everlasting life.

The Śvetasvataropanisad firmly declares that there is no other way to reach there. (**Nà anya panthā vidyate ayanāya...**) [We have to come back to this verse later.] This way unites heaven and earth together. It means that it unites man on earth and the Holy God Almighty in heaven. Thus Jesus became a peace-bridge between heaven and earth. The angels sang the song of peace when He came down to the earth: "...on earth peace to men on whom His favour rests." (Luke 2:14) After He had completed His mission on earth (His crucifixion and resurrection), He appeared to His disciples offering this peace: **"Peace be with you."** (John 20:20; 21;26) Yes, Jesus is the peace-bridge, the way connecting heaven to earth through which we enter into the presence of the living God. There is no other way like this and therefore this is the supreme way. The **Upaniṣads** say that **Guru** is the way. Jesus boldly proclaims that He is the **Guru** and the **Way** and there is no other **Guru** or **Way** to reach heaven.

(4) Guru Himself Is the Supreme Knowledge (Gurureva parā vidya)

'Vidya' means knowledge. The words **vidya** and **veda** originate from the Sanskrit root **'vid'** which means to know, understand, to learn etc. **Vidya** is the key-word in Vedic literature. Whatever is opposite to **vidya** is called **avidya.** Whoever follows **avidya** is in utter darkness of death. But **vidya** will give us eternal life.[145] In fact, the real **vidya** (knowledge) is to know **Puruṣa** who is the way to everlasting life. The **Upaniṣads** named this knowledge as the supreme knowledge. **Guru** is the person who gives the supreme knowledge. But here, **Guru** and **vidya** are the same person since it is written **Guru** Himself is the supreme knowledge. The knowledge which the **Guru** gives is not a philosophy or a doctrine which stands itself without the **Guru.** But the knowledge which **Guru** gives is the supreme knowledge -- that is **Guru** Himself in the totality of His personality. Look at what the Holy Spirit has recorded about Jesus in the New Testament:

". . . we are in Christ Jesus, who has become for us wisdom from God..." (1. Corinthians 1:30)

Again it is written for us *"to know the mystery of God, namely Christ, in whom are hidden all the treasures of wisdom and knowledge."* (Colossians 2: 2,3)

The knowledge about Christ, the mystery of God, is superior to any other knowledge of the world. Understanding this mystery St. Paul writes:

> *"But whatever was to my profit I now consider loss for the sake of Christ. What is more, I consider everything a loss compared to the surpassing greatness of knowing Christ Jesus my Lord, for whose sake I have lost all things."* (Philippians 3:7,8)

St. Paul also wants each and every one of us to know the excellency of the supreme knowledge. We see this in his continuous prayer on our behalf:

"I keep asking that the God of our Lord Jesus Christ, the glorious Father, may give you the Spirit of wisdom and revelation, so that you may KNOW HIM better." (Ephesians 1:17)

Yes, Jesus Himself is the Supreme Knowledge (**parā vidya).** Following Him is eternal life. And this is that most excellent good news that must be proclaimed all over the world.

(5) Guru Himself is the Supreme Journey (Gurureva parāyaṇam)

The word **'ayaṇam'** originally means going or walking. **Parāyaṇam** is a compound word which can be split into **para + ayanam.** A famous Indian myth is entitled **Rāmāyaṇam (Rama + ayaṇam)** which is usually translated as the journey of Rama. But in the word **parāyaṇam, 'para'** is not a person but it indicates the state of superiority as we have seen it earlier. Therefore we can translate the word **parāyaṇam** as the supreme journey. According to the **Upaniṣads** the supreme journey is the **Guru** Himself.

When the sages waited for the **Niṣkalanka Puruṣa** (Sinless and Perfect Man) they were expecting in Him a perfect example to follow. The Lord Jesus Christ set an example for mankind to follow. Whatever He taught His disciples was from His own life and from His own personality. For the disciples of Jesus learning from Him was walking with Him. By the Supreme way the **Guru** Himself went ahead and then He commanded His disciples to follow His footsteps. To walk with Jesus in the path of eternity is definitely the supreme journey.

Until Jesus gave the Sermon on the Mount, the world did not hear the message to love their enemies and pray for them. (Matthew 5:43,44) Jesus could sincerely love His enemies even at the time He received the bitter cup from them. He washed the feet of His disciples including Judas even though He knew that he was the one going to betray Him. When He had finished washing their feet Jesus asked them:

> "Do you understand what I have done for you?"

Then He explained:

> "You call Me 'Teacher' (Guru) and 'Lord,' and rightly so,
> for that is what I am. Now that I,
> your Lord and Teacher, have washed your feet, you
> also should wash one another's feet. I have set
> you an example that you should do as I have done for you."
> (John 13: 12-15)

Whatever He taught He practiced even on His sacrificial pillar on the mount of Golgotha. At the time He accepted the cross from His enemies He prayed for them: *"Father, forgive them, for they do not know what they are doing.*" (Luke 23:34) When we walk with Jesus we have to identify with Jesus in everything. Today people love to study the Word of Jesus and they love to preach the Word and many of them are even willing to fast and pray for days and months. But they find difficulty in forgiving their enemies and loving them and earnestly praying for them. It is simply because they are not walking with our **Guru** the Lord Jesus Christ.

Jesus said:

"It is enough for the disciple that he be as his ***Master (Guru)****."* (Matthew 10:25. KJV)

If we fully surrendered ourselves to the lordship of the **Guru,** spontaneously and automatically we would produce fruit. Then we would think with the mind of Christ and our actions would follow from thoughts originating in the Master's mind. This is our ultimate aim - to be like Jesus. But without the help of **Guru** the disciple cannot attain to the maturity of his Master. That is what Jesus said: **"Apart from Me you can do nothing."** (John 15:5) The Master's will is to bring every disciple to the full maturity of the Master. **"Present everyone perfect in Christ"** is the will of the Lord for every believer. (Colossians 1:28) However, even after the disciple reaches maturity, *Guru will be Guru forever. The disciple will be like the Master but he will not be the Master. As long as he walks with Guru he is like Guru but the moment he loses contact with the Guru he will fall down like the branch which separates from the tree.*

What is Unmanifested (Avyakta)?

When we know **Puruṣa** as our **Guru** and start to walk with Him, we will know what is the unmanifested part **(avyakta)** in the faculty of man. In the verses we quoted earlier from the **Kaṭhopaniṣad** (chapter 3: 10,11 and chapter 6: 7,8) we can see this unmanifested part of man as superior to soul and subordinate to **Puruṣa.** This part of man was not revealed to the sages before the crucifixion of the Lord Jesus Christ. So the sage who wrote the verses simply named it **avyakta** (unmanifested). However, when we look at a man after he has received Jesus as his Saviour and Lord and Master we will see that this part starts to develop in him. Through Jesus, the Son of God, we have the right to become children of God. St. John writes in his first Epistle:

> *"How great is the love the Father has lavished on us, that we should be called children of God!*

> *And that is what we are! ... Dear friends, now we are children of God and what we will be* ***has not yet been made known. But we know that when He appears we shall be like Him."*** (1.John 3:1- 2)

The verses state today's condition of the children of God. At the same time they say that tomorrow's condition is not yet fully manifested in us. But the word of God says that tomorrow when we see Jesus face to face, we shall be like Him. That means we will be fully transformed to the image of Christ. That is going to be manifested on that day. But before the crucifixion of Jesus it was totally unmanifested for the sages. Still when God gave them the revelation about the total man they could recognize this unrevealed part and they named it **'avyakta'**.

The Four Stages of Salvation in the Process of Transformation

God Almighty called His people to be conformed to the likeness of His Son. This transformation does not happen to a believer in a day. It is a daily process in our life. According to **Vedic** literature, there are four stages of salvation: **sālokya, sāmīpya, sārūpya and sāyūjya.**

The word **sālokya** comes from **sa** + **loka** which signifies the believer is admitted into the sphere (world) of God by faith in the Word of God. Like a newborn baby the believer is just entering into this sphere of God.

In the next stage he has a strong desire to go near to the Lord and obtain more knowledge of salvation. They have to drink the spiritual milk, the word of God, for their growth. For that they have to go near to God, more and more. The sages called this stage of salvation **'sāmīpya'**. This name originated from the word **'samīpa'** which means proximity (nearness in space and time) to **Puruṣa** the author of salvation. The person who is saved will experience constant fellowship with the Lord Jesus Christ. He knows that the Lord is very near to him as a continuous help in trouble. We who experience this salvation have the precious promise from the Lord Jesus Christ: *"And surely I am with you always, to the very end of the age."* (Matthew 28:20)

The next stage is **sārūpya.** It is from **sa** + **rūpa** which means sameness or similitude in form. In this stage of salvation we are identifying with the Saviour in every aspect. We have already seen in the second part of the book that we are identified with different aspects of **Puruṣa-Prajāpati's** sacrifice. Here, we are identifying with the death, the burial and the resurrection of the Lord Jesus Christ. St. Paul writes:

> ***"Now if we died with Christ, we believe that we will also live with Him. . . The death He died, He died to sin once for all; but the life He lives, He lives to God. In the same way, count yourselves dead to sin but alive to God in Christ Jesus."*** (Romans 6:8-11)

The fourth stage is **sāyūjya.** This word comes from **sa** + **yuj** which means intimate union or communion. In this stage the devotee enters into union with **Puruṣa.**

When St. Paul wanted to write about the visions and revelations he introduced himself in an indirect way:

"I know a man in Christ. . . (2.Corinthians 12:2)

In this stage the devotee is completely immersed in the personality of Christ. In other words, the Lord Jesus Christ Himself envelopes him with His personality and the world can see in him Christ only.

When you know **Puruṣa** as your **Guru** and you start to follow Him, God begins to work in you. You are ordained by God to be conformed to the image of **Puruṣa,** the Lord Jesus Christ who came from heaven. The process of the work of transformation starts the very first day you receive **Puruṣa** as your **Guru.** From this time onwards man has a special part in him in addition to his senses of the body, mind, intellect, and soul. The ancient sages called the part of man **'avyakta'** (unmanifested) because it was not revealed to them. But now it is manifested. Therefore we have to re-name this part. I would give the name: **Image of Puruṣa the Christ.**

In the light of this revelation we can summarise the ideas expressed in the **Kaṭhopaniṣad** from chapter 3, verses 10,11 and chapter 6, verses 7,8 as follows:

Man on earth has to know Puruṣa, the Lord of immortality, with his five senses for life eternal. But the five senses have limitations and therefore the senses have to receive the assistance of their superiors.

The sense-objects (the experiences like seeing, hearing etc.) are superior to the senses. Therefore by experience we have to know Puruṣa for Mukti. Experience will be alive and active only by the assistance of the mind and therefore mind is superior to the senses-objects. Mind is also incapable of comprehending heavenly knowledge of eternal life. So the mind has to be devoted to Puruṣa under the guidance of the intellect which is superior to the mind. At the same time the intellect will also fail to grasp divine knowledge without the help of its superiors. Soul is superior to intellect but the soul will not be active without its Master. Who is the master of the soul? This part of man was not manifested earlier but now it is revealed. It is called the image of Puruṣa, the Christ. The image of Puruṣa will not work itself without its Master. Who is superior to the image of Puruṣa? He is Puruṣa the Christ Himself, the real Man of the image. This Puruṣa is present in His creation. None is superior to Puruṣa. He is the Supreme and the ultimate. He is the Supreme Way. He is the supreme goal of man on this earth. For eternal life the total man has to surrender himself to the Lordship of Puruṣa - the Son of Man Jesus Christ. One who knows Him will never die. He will live eternally.

Jesus said:

"I am the resurrection and the life. He who believes in Me will live, even though he dies; and whoever lives and believes in Me will never die." (John 11:25).

The Spirit of Puruṣa and Faith

Faith is very important for obtaining salvation. But without the Spirit of **Puruṣa** nobody can believe in the glorious message of redemption. Those who believe in this message are saved and they begin to testify about **Puruṣa.** In order to believe in something people need direct experience of vision or hearing. To witness about **Puruṣa** is the next step which is totally impossible for anybody if he is not present on the scene to see and grasp things with his senses. To testify or to witness are the legal terms constantly used in the courts. The court will not give any validity to a witness who is not present on the scene or is giving second hand information.

But how can man of this century see the act of creation or the act of redemption which happened long ago? Our eyes, ears, mind and intellect were absent at the time of creation of the world and the redemptive sacrifice on the cross. In other words, we did not see those things. Then how can we stand as a witness to the redemptive sacrifice of **Puruṣa?** Who was present there to witness the truth? Can you know who was there in person? *The Spirit of Puruṣa was there at the scene of creation and redemption.* When He created the heavens and the earth the Spirit of the Lord was hovering over the waters (Genesis 1:2) *"Through Him all things were made; without Him nothing was made that has been made."* (John 1:3) In the redemptive sacrifice on the cross **Puruṣa** Himself was the sacrificial victim. Therefore **Puruṣa** has to give us the direct witness of the events for our faith. The Spirit of **Puruṣa** witnesses to our soul and intellect and mind what the Lord has done for the salvation of the world. When we know this **Puruṣa** as the supreme authority and the intimate part of our being we experience everything as if we were personally present there on the scene. Here we do not have any doubt about the account of creation or in the nature the redemptive sacrifice on the cross. Since **Puruṣa** is the supreme part of the believer he can legally give witness to the redemptive sacrifice of **Puruṣa.** That is the reason why Jesus commanded us: "You also must testify, for you have been with me from the beginning." (John 15:27) Praise God for such a blessed assurance of eternal life that the Lord has given to us.

As the **Advayatarakopanisad** continues its description about **Guru**, the Lord Jesus Christ Himself is the supreme peak (climax) of every good thing and therefore He Himself is the Supreme wealth to achieve. (**Gurureva parākāṣta, Gurureva paraṃ dhanaṃ...**) Jesus asks: "What is a man profited, if he shall gain the whole world, and lose his soul." (Matthew 16:26).

Chapter 18

MANY WAYS AND THE ONE WAY

According to modern Hinduism there are many ways of salvation. They believe that eventually all of them reach heaven as every river flows to the ocean. As the Hindu philosophers often say, Hinduism can tolerate and even accept all other religious thought and still it can keep its own identity. Jawaharlal Nehru, the first Prime Minister of India, was right when he wrote: "Hinduism as faith is vague, amorphous, many sided, all things to all men."[146] Normally, Hindus do not have any difficulty accepting Jesus as one among the many but most of them do not agree with the statement that Jesus is the one and the only way of salvation.

What do the Vedas and the Upaniṣads say?

Let us quote a very important verse from the **Śvetāśvataropaniṣad:**

"Vedāhametam puruṣaṃ mahāntam

ādityavarṇaṃ tamasaḥ parastāt

tameva viditvati mṛtumeti

nānyaḥ panthā vidyate-ayanāya." [147]

(I know the mighty Puruṣa of the colour of the sun beyond the darkness. Only in knowing Him does one pass over death. **There is no other path leading to eternal life.**)

We can see the same verse in the **Yajur Veda** in the concluding part of the **Puruṣasūkta.** In both places **Puruṣa** is of the colour of the sun and distant from darkness. It simply means He is light and the destroyer of darkness. We have already seen who this light of the world is who destroys the darkness of sin.

The verse concludes in the **Puruṣasūkta** as follows:

> **"tameva vidvānamṛta iha bhavati**
> **nānyaḥ panthā ayanāya vedyate"**[148]

(Thus one who knows this becomes able to reach the state of deathlessness. No other way is known for this.)

Here we see that the **Upaniṣads** and the **Vedas** unanimously proclaim that the way to the land of eternal life is to know the **Puruṣa.** They also declare that there is no other way to reach there. We have seen that the main theme of the **Puruṣasūkta** is the sacrifice of the **Puruṣa-Prajāpati** which is for the remission of the sin of mankind. In conclusion, the **Puruṣasūkta** confirms the message by proclaiming that there is no other way for salvation of mankind. Moreover, we see the name of this way given by the sages throughout **Vedic** literature is: **Parāgati (The Supreme Way).** The word **para** or **supreme** means the highest or the climax and this alone is the ultimate. There cannot be two **supreme ways** at the same time.

Then, What about the Four Ways of Salvation?

From ancient times onwards we have heard that **karma** (actions), **jñāna** (knowledge), **yoga** (concentration of mind) and **bhakti** (devotion or love) are the means to the attainment of **Mukti** or **Mokṣa.** Let us briefly go through each of these one by one.

(1) The Way of Works (Karmamārga)

The word **'karma'** means work, deed, action etc. The **karma mārga** (the way of works) is the most popular way of salvation in the world. The **yajña** (sacrifice) is considered as the highest **karma.** Therefore, **karma mārga** is also known as **yajña mārga.** M. Dhavamony writes:

"In the Vedic period sacrifice was considered a mystical sacrament of redemption, . .Man was identified with his sacrifice . . .

Redemption is first of all from death and then from sin."[149] Mr. Dhavamony quotes the **Sathapathabrahmana** at this point:

"Man, as soon as he is born, is born in person as a debt due to death; when he sacrifices, he redeems his person from death." [150]

We have studied the predominance of sacrifice in the first two parts of this book. Actually **karma mārga** originated from sacrifice. Sacrifice is an action of man to obtain salvation. It is also true that we have numerous verses in the **Vedas** to support the idea of obtaining salvation by the act of sacrifice. However, we have studied in detail that all those Vedic and Old Testament sacrifices were just mere shadows of the original sacrifice of the **Puruṣa Prajāpati** which originated in the heart of God even before the foundation of the world. And also we have seen that the perfect sacrifice of God was completely fulfilled in the crucifixion and the resurrection of Jesus Christ. Man could not be justified by the imperfect works of sacrifices performed by man. Therefore salvation is not based on the work of man. Jesus presented Himself to God as the sinless atoning Lamb and only through His perfect work are we able to enter into eternal life. So along with the **Upaniṣads** we say:

"Vedāhametam puruṣaṃ . . . Na anya panthā vidyate-ayanāya."

(I know the Puruṣa.... There is no other way to go to the land of eternal life.")

Today people are trying to do many good works for salvation without knowing **Puruṣa-Prajāpati's** perfect sacrifice. The Holy Bible says, **"All our righteous deeds are like filthy rags."** (Isaiah 64:6) In fact nobody can do good works without the Spirit of the **Puruṣa.** Jesus said to us: **"Without Me you can do nothing."** (John 15:5) At the same time we will automatically produce good fruit if we join together with the tree who came down from heaven. We have studied this in the second part of this book as the living sacrifice which is the fourth phase of sacrifice.

Side-Effects of Karma Doctrine

Even though the doctrine of **karma** originated from the performance of sacrifice, many other deep-rooted ideas and beliefs are formed in the lives of people as side-effects of this doctrine. It began as a belief that **karma** is an inevitable degrading power upon the soul. It is not possible to escape from the effects of **karma.** Because of this, man has to suffer in this world for man's **karma** (deed) is evil. It is sin. It will not leave him alone. Acharya Daya Prakash Titus explains this view beautifully quoting the great epic The Mahabhārata:

> "Just as the calf of a cow would find its own mother out of a thousand other cows, so also the **karma** would never miss the right person to whom it may belong."

The author continues: "In other words, **karma** is stamped on the head of every human being, and the destiny of the soul is ceaselessly determined thereby. . . Belief in the cycle of **karma** over a period of nearly three thousand years has had some decisive effects upon the lifestyle of our country, for good or bad. But it has produced the relinquishment of one's unseen fate."[151]

Acharya Daya Prakash further points out that this fatalism leads people to laziness and indifference to the misery of others. They believe that sufferings are due to **karma** (man's action, sin) and no one can alter his fate. Finally, he says, "the doctrine of **karma** pathetically postpones, or puts off, any serious attempt by the soul for liberation from spiritual bondage and realization of **mokṣa** in this very life, believing that **mokṣa** would, any way, come along his or her course, one day or other, in the great cycle of re-birth - even though it may be after one million years."[152]

By this they forget the truth that man has only one life on this earth and after that he has to spend his eternity in heaven or in hell. Dr. P. J. Titus, another author, writes in his article, Karma and the Cross, : "Within the whole system of karmic philosophy there is no idea of a theology of love and forgiveness and grace of God. When a man is eternally bound to his own wheel of **karma,** how can he escape?" [153]

Against this background, the good news of salvation shines brightly. "**Now is the time of God's favour, now is the day of salvation.**" (2 Corinthians 6: 2) "**Through Christ Jesus the law of the Spirit of life sets me free from the law of sin (karma) and death.**" (Romans 8: 2)

As Dr.Titus writes: "For what the law of **karma** could not do, Jesus Christ completed on the cross of Calvary. He declared, "**it is finished.**" (John 19:30) All humanistic self-salvation projects have been eliminated through the substitutionary atonement of Jesus

Christ. Man need not work to earn salvation."[154] It does not mean that we do not have to do any good works. In fact, we are redeemed from dead works to do good works. We do good because we have come to the knowledge of **Puruṣa** and have been redeemed.

(2) The Way of Knowledge (Jñānamārga)

The **Mahābhārata** also points out the release from the bondage of **karma**:

> **"Karmanā badhyate janturvidyayā tu pramucyate"**[155]
> (Souls are bound by karma and released by knowledge.)

What is the subject of knowledge? What or whom do we have to know? The **Vedas** and **Upaniṣads** unanimously say that we have to know the **Puruṣa** who has sacrificed His life for us. We have seen that **Puruṣa** is the supreme knowledge (**parāvidya**) to travel through the supreme way to achieve the supreme goal.

(3) The Way of Yoga (The Way of Mind-Concentration)

The word **'yoga'** originates from the Sanskrit root **yuj** which means **joins**, or **unites** with something or somebody. So **'yoga'** originally means **union**. V. S. Apte's Sanskrit English Dictionary gives all these meanings along with the following explanation: "Deep and abstract meditation, concentration of the mind, contemplation of the Supreme Spirit." This is the original purpose of the way of the **yoga.** There is only one answer in the **Vedas and the Upaniṣads** when the question is asked on whom we must concentrate our attention; **Puruṣa,** the Almighty. We have already discussed this aspect from the **Kaṭhopaniṣad.** The Vedas further point out three important stages of meditation:

(1) **Śravaṇa** (Hearing about God from the Guru),
(2) **Manana** (keeping on thinking about what he has heard),
(3) **Nididhyāsana** (profound and repeated meditation on the word of God and dwelling in Him).

The Holy Bible also promotes the teaching of meditation. *"Blessed is the man ... whose delight is in the law of the Lord, on His law he meditates day and night."* Thus the book of Psalms begins. The Psalmists were always meditators. Asaph sings: *"I will meditate on all your works and consider all your mighty deeds"* (Psalm 77:12). In the solitude of the wilderness King David meditated upon the Word of God. We hear his songs of meditation in Psalm 63: *"When I remember Thee upon my bed, and meditate on Thee in the night watches, my soul shall be satisfied as with marrow and fatness; and my mouth shall praise Thee with joyful lips."* (verses 5,6)

Today's TM Movements and the Modern Yogis

However, today's Transcendental Meditation groups are not traveling towards that goal because they miss **Puruṣa,** the central personality and targeting point of the meditation. Modern meditation is just opposite of Vedic principles for the Vedas say to meditate on **Puruṣa** with all your mind, intellect and soul. At the same time modern TM concentrates its meditation on nothing. In other words, they give people training to evacuate their minds.

A research study reveals that over one million Americans are involved in Transcendental Meditation.[156] Josh McDowell writes: "As I have traveled throughout North America and Europe, I have observed this explosive growth of interest in the East... One can hardly walk across a university campus and not see the advertising of the TM movement"[157] Maharishi Mahesh Yogi, who brought TM to North America, says: "Transcendental Meditation is the only way to salvation and success in life; there is no other way."[158] The North American newspapers have published several articles on Maharishi and his TM. Recently through the American news media Maharishi invited all the governments of the world to TM through which he offers "heaven on earth."[159]

The Secret of Transcendental Meditation

Maharishi offers salvation and heaven on this earth through TM. This is very attractive and colourful. TM temporarily diminishes the pain of sin and suppresses its guilt. Maharishi says: "TM develops all the seven states of consciousness in the individual, and develops a perfect man with the ability to employ natural law to work for him and achieve anything he wants. The seven states of consciousness are:

(1) Waking - **Jāgrata cetana**
(2) Dreaming - **Swapna cetana**
(3) Sleeping - **Suṣupti cetana**
(4) Transcendental consciousness - **Tūrya cetana**
(5) Cosmic consciousness - **Tūryateet cetana**
(6) God consciousness - **Bhagavat cetana**
(7) Unity consciousness - **Braḥmi cetana."** [160]

These seven states are not substantiated by any writings from the **Vedas** or the **Upaniṣads** even though the advertisement says it is the result of "Maharishi's Vedic Science and Technology".

It is true that TM can drive people through these seven states of consciousness and reduce stress in their life. But we have to know the real cause of the stress and recognize its source. The stress is developed in a human being due to the agony of the guilt of sin. TM works like a pain-pill or a tranquilizer in that the pain is not felt by the patient. Some of the modern psychiatrists and medical doctors in our hospitals started to give this pill to their patients. They began to advise them to go for TM.[161]

Let us see how it works in a normal man.

A man in his waking state of consciousness (**jāgrata cetana**) goes for TM treatment. He has mental pain and agonies and has no peace and no rest. His mind is awake and he feels pain. The pain is not the result of his imagination but it is real and normal. This pain and restlessness are symptoms of the real sickness, sin. Because of the restlessness man seeks a permanent place for his rest. Therefore, it is also normal that he seeks for deliverance from pain. TM leads him into the second state, that is, dreaming (**swapna cetana**) according to Maharishi. In the first state, his mind is awake and alert but in the second state the mind is in a state of drowsiness or half-sleep. Still the mind will work through dreams. Here, the mind becomes involved in sweet or horrible dream experiences but both are unreal. (But the real truth-seekers pray that they might be led from unreal to the real.) In the second state also man feels the pain of sin in an indirect way. Therefore, TM leads him to the third state of consciousness and that is called '**deep sleep (suṣupti)**'. In this stage he does not feel much pain from his sin. When we are in deep sleep we forget all our worries. Our mind, intellect and other inner faculties also relax along with our body. Similarly TM can bring people into this state even though it is not a natural sleep. However, man cannot silence his guilty conscience forever. From sleep he has to wake up. But TM brings people from there to four other deeper states of consciousness in succession. From deep sleep he goes into transcendental consciousness and from there he enters three other deeper experiences of so-called cosmic and god-consciousness and unity consciousness. In this final stage he feels he is '100% Divine'. Here, he even dares to say that he is God. Thus TM ultimately supports the **Sāmkhya** and **Vedānta** philosophy of Hinduism.

But man has to face reality. He cannot silence the cry of his soul forever. When he comes to his normal wake up condition he again realizes the real pain of his soul. That is the reason why people are taught to practice TM daily and are in fact, encouraged to keep themselves in their meditative mood throughout the day. If they could completely heal the disease of sin there would be no awareness of pain and there would be no need for the continuing TM practice. As he continues this routine daily he gradually enters a state of decreasing activity. And even though he continues TM throughout his life, he still has to come back to his state of consciousness before he dies. It is commonly noticed that the people who are even insane will come back to their normal condition before they face death. TM is not a remedy for the stress of mankind. It is just like giving pain-pills to cancer patients without curing the actual disease.

The Side-effects of TM

Pat Means points out some side-effects of TM. He writes:

"Recent studies reported in **Psychology Today** have indicated that TM may have the side effect of decreasing our ability to think creatively. This side effect is common to most forms of eastern meditation because they supposedly 'transcend' conscious thought."[162] It will lead one to spiritual dullness. By this one will lose his ability to grasp the truth. This is the most serious effect of the TM movement. TM can open a person to demonic activity as Pat Means mentions in his book. He writes: "The danger here comes from combining the mental passivity of the meditation state with the active repetition of the **mantra.**"[163] The chanter does not understand the meaning of **mantra** and he just repeats it with his lips without the active participation of the mind or intellect. According to Maharishi the purpose of this chanting is *"to produce an effect in another world; to draw the attention of those higher beings or gods living there."* [164] And also we see that the final state of consciousness is the feeling that man is God. Maharishi writes in one of his books, "Although we are all 100% divine consciously we do not know that we are divine." [165] Only through TM we reach this knowledge, according to Maharishi. It reminds us of the thought of the ex-angel Lucifer, the king of the Satanic kingdom, as recorded in the book of Isaiah and in the book of Ezekiel: *"I will ascend above the tops of the clouds; I will make myself like the Most High."* (Isaiah 14:14). *"In the pride of your heart you say, 'Iam god'..."* (Ezekiel 28:2) That was the cause of his fall from heaven to hell.

The True Yoga - Union with God

Although the word '**yoga**' means union with God or the concentrating of the mind on God, the practice of TM drives people away from God to the opposite direction. We have seen earlier in chapter 17, under the sub-title <u>The Four Stages of Salvation in the Process of Transformation,</u> in what way we can unite with God. The fourth stage **sāyujya** deals with this. (**sa+yuj** is **sayujya** which means intimate union). Union with God is possible through **Puruṣa,** His beloved Son Jesus Christ. Without **Puruṣa** no one knows God. In order to reach this unity with God we have to travel in precisely the opposite direction to TM. For the realization of God, the **Kaṭhopaniṣad** shouts and says: **"Uttiṣtata jāgrata"** which means **arise** and **keep awake**. TM wants to bring us from the state of waking to the state of dreaming and sleeping but the ancient sage boldly tells us to awake from our sleep and keep on watching for attaining salvation. We have to be very alert and to be vigilant. In the sixteenth chapter of this book we have discussed the important role of the mind in order to know the mighty **Puruṣa** for salvation. We have also heard the voice of the **Bṛhadāraṇyakopaniṣad: "By mind we see and by mind we hear."** We have to search His Way, Truth and Light with all our five senses. Mind, body and soul with all other faculties must remain in a state of active consciousness. In fact, it is just the opposite way of TM teaching.

When a normal person comes into the presence of God in a state of waking consciousness at first he may feel double his pain. It is just because he sees his real pathetic situation and unworthiness in the light of the holiness of God. Remembering his sin and his separation from God due to his sin he begins to cry. This cry is normal and healthy even though it is bitter. This genuine sorrow is repentance which leads him to the Saviour. Here he discovers his inability to cover up his sin and escape from its power. As the result of this he strongly feels that he needs the Saviour to save him from the situation. As soon as he finds

Him, the **Puruṣa,** the Saviour, as his Lord and **Guru** he will enter into a never ending state of happiness. This will be experienced by him in his normal conscious state. As the days pass by he will know this **Puruṣa** more and more and his state of happiness also will be increased more and more. For obtaining this he does not have to do anything but to receive Him with an open mind. Once he knows the **Puruṣa** he is already admitted to the sphere of eternal salvation and happiness on the basis of the quality of the finished work of **Puruṣa** - that is His eternal sacrifice. This first stage of salvation is called, **"sālokya"** as we have seen earlier. In the second stage, **'sāmīpya'** we enjoy a sense of the nearness of His presence. The third,**'sārūpya'** is the identification stage. The fourth one is the **'sāyujya'** in which we completely immerse in Him. This is the real union with God. When St. Paul begins to explain his mystical experience he writes about himself: **"I know a man in Christ."** (2.Cor.12:2)The expression **"in Christ"** occurs many places in the letters of St. Paul such as *"live in harmony in the Lord"* (Phil. 4: 2), *"rejoice in the Lord"* (Phil.4: 4), *"fallen asleep in Jesus"* (1.Thess. 4: 15) etc. As James Stewart writes, "The heart of Paul's religion is union with Christ."[166]

In order to reach this ultimate stage of salvation we must meditate on **Puruṣa** the Lord Jesus Christ. For that the **Upaniṣads** and the Holy Bible tell us to **wake up (uttiṣṭata jāgrata)** and listen to the word of God.[167] St. James tells us: *"Accept the word planted in you, which can save you."* (James 1:21) This is the first stage of meditation, **'śravana'** (hearing) according to the Vedas. The book of Hebrews chapter 2 starts with this: "We must pay more careful attention to what we have heard." The sages call this second stage **`manana'** (keep on thinking about what we have heard). Chapter 3 continues to say: "Therefore, holy brothers, who share in the heavenly calling, FIX YOUR THOUGHTS ON JESUS." (verse 1) Let our minds dwell on Jesus. This is the final stage of meditation **`Nididhyāsana'** (profound and repeated meditation of the word of God (Jesus) and dwelling in the word (Jesus).

> "Finally, brethren, (let your minds dwell on these things:)
> whatever is true (Jesus is the truth) ,
> whatever is honorable (Jesus is the most honorable),
> whatever is just (Jesus is the ultimate justice),
> whatever is pure (Jesus is pure and spotless),
> whatever is lovely (Jesus is the most beautiful),
> whatever is of good repute (Jesus is of the most excellent reputation)

if there is any virtue (Jesus is supremely virtuous),
if any thing is worthy of praise (Jesus is most worthy to be praised)!
THINK ON THESE THINGS. (Philippians 4:8).

This is the true **Yoga** in which we have filled our minds with the best and the supreme goodness. This is the way to eternal life. While TM requires us to evacuate our minds and leads us into a dream state, deep sleep and finally to death, true Yoga fills our minds with God and leads us to everlasting life.

(4) The Way of Bhakti (The Way of Devotion or Love)

The literal meaning of **bhakti** is devotion or faithfulness. But Hindu scholars often translate this word as love. Certainly, this love is spiritual. Swami Nikhilananda writes on this as follows: "Spiritual love, or **bhakti,** is directed only to God, whose effulgence (brilliance) puts to shame 'a million suns, a million moons, and a million gods of beauty.' "[168]

Some of the philosophers consider that this is a fourth way of salvation. But on close observation we discover this is not a fourth way of salvation but just one of the parts of the one way. For salvation we have to concentrate our mind on **Puruṣa** with **bhakti** (love) and diligently seek Him. In this way we will find Him and know Him and will then continue to love and serve Him. We do good works (**karma**) not because the Law demands it but because it comes automatically and spontaneously on the basis of the knowledge of **Puruṣa's love** towards us. This is the way of immortality.

The Four Ways Are One Way

From our discussion it is very clear that the **Vedas** and **Upaniṣads** never taught four ways of salvation. They are all four aspects of the one way of salvation. Swami Nikhilananda also supports this view. He writes:

"A man's action may be compared to the flight of a bird, which needs three things -- two wings and a tail -- for its graceful movement. By means of the wings it balances itself in the air, and by the tail, like a rudder in a boat, it keeps its course. In a worker, love and knowledge are two wings, and meditation the tail. When these function harmoniously, the action becomes graceful." [169]

In order to know Him, the **Puruṣa**, we have to seek Him with all our being, concentrating our mind on Him. So we see **jñāna mārga** and **yoga mārga** are uniting together. If we know Him we have to follow in His footsteps and produce the fruit of sacrifice in this period of our being a living sacrifice as St. Paul writes in Romans 12:1-2. Here **karma mārga** works together with the way of knowledge and the way of concentration. The Holy Bible says that faith (knowledge) without deeds is useless. St. James writes: "Was not our ancestor Abraham considered righteous for what he did when he offered his son Isaac on the altar? You see his faith (knowledge) and his actions were working together, and his faith was made complete by what he did." (James 2:21,22) We offer our lives as a living sacrifice but not because the law requires it of us. Most willingly we follow Him because of the covenant of love. We experience His great love and from that divine love we love Him and others. Thus the way of love (**bhakti-marga**) also works together along with the other three ways. When we start to walk with Him in the supreme way of eternal life we immediately understand these four ways are not separate ways but are united in a single way to heaven. Now we are able to understand better the significance of the Vedic proclamation: "Only knowing Him, the Purusa, does one pass over death. There is no other path leading to eternal life."[170]

The Holy Bible Also Proclaims the One Way

We have already seen that the Holy Bible also proclaims this same way for salvation. In conclusion we recall the words in the prayer of Jesus: "Now this is eternal life: that they may know You (Heavenly Father), the only true God, and Jesus Christ, whom You have sent." (John 17:3).

Jesus Christ says: "I am the way and the truth and the life. No one comes to the Father except through Me." (John 14:6).

St.Peter proclaims: "Salvation is found in no one else, for there is no other name under heaven given to men by which we must be saved." (Acts 4:12).

St. Paul writes: "For there is one God and one mediator between God and men, the Man (Puruṣa) Christ Jesus, who gave Himself as a ransom for all men- the testimony given in its proper time." (1.Timothy 2:5)

Chapter 19

THE MAN - PURUṢA - CHRIST JESUS, THE MEASURING ROD

The Man with a Measuring Rod in His Hand

The prophet Ezekiel in the Old Testament saw in his visions a Man who measured the temple of God with a measuring rod in his hand. This Man instructed him:

> *"Son of man, look with your eyes, and hear with your ears and pay attention to everything I am going to show you, for that is why you have been brought here. Tell the house of Israel everything you see."* (Ezekiel 40:4).

Ezekiel is devoted to God and he faithfully receives messages from Him alone. He also knows that a prophet is a mouth-piece of God. The servant of God is not to be instructed or guided by any man and he is not supposed to preach man's message. He just delivers the message and faithfully proclaims, **"Thus the Lord says"** or **"the word of the Lord came to me..."** (Ezekiel 38:1) So who is the Man here, with a measuring rod in His hand? Who is He to teach the servant of God and tell him to go and preach the message to the children of Israel?

It is clear from the context that this Man "whose appearance was like bronze" is not an ordinary man. Ezekiel devoted 8 chapters (40-47) to this Man in his prophetical book. This Man measured the temple of God with the rod in His hand. He measured every part of the temple. He measured the wall. (40: 5) He measured the threshold of the gate. (40: 6) He measured the portico of the gateway. (40: 8) He measured the width of the entrance to the gateway (40:11), and the gateway from the top of the rear wall . . .(40:13) From chapter 40 to

47, we can read at least 23 times He measured various parts of the temple and even the spiritual river which begins to flow from the temple of God. (chapter 47)

Thus He measured the temple and set the standard and permanent design for the temple of God.

The Man said to the prophet:

"Son of man, describe the temple to the people of Israel, that they may be ashamed of their sins. Let them consider the plan, and if they are ashamed of all they have done, make known to them the design of the temple - its arrangement, its exits and entrances -- its whole design and all its regulations and laws. Write these down before them so that they may be faithful to its design and follow all its regulations. This is the law of the temple: All the surrounding area on top of the mountain will be most holy. Such is the law of the temple." (43:10-12).

Which is the Temple of God?

When we look into the subject in the light of New Testament revelation we can easily understand that God's temple on earth is not a man-made building. St.Paul writes to the believers of Corinth:

"Don't you know that you yourselves are God's temple and that God's Spirit lives in you. If anyone destroys God's temple, God will destroyhim; for God's temple is sacred, and you are that temple." (1.Corinthians 3:16,17)

God led Israel to build the temple literally two times. God wants to manifest and even share His holiness with His people. But the people performed everything outwardly without spiritual understanding. However, God Himself allowed the earthly temple buildings to be destroyed. The temple was the demonstration of the holiness of God. But the holiness of God may never be shared by a man-made building. St.Stephen makes exactly this point in his sermon: "It was Solomon who built the house for Him. However, the Most High does not live in houses made by men." (Acts 7:47, 48) God wants to live among His people. St.Paul writes in another place:

"For we are the temple of the living God. As God has said: ' I will live with them and walk among them, and I will be their God, and they will be my people." (2.Corinthians 6:16)

It is a great mystery and blessing that the Holy God dwells in a human soul. We are sharing His holiness. As we read in the book of Ephesians:

"Praise be to the God and Father of our Lord Jesus Christ who has blessed us in heavenly realms with every spiritual blessing in Christ. For He chose us in Him before the creation of the world **to be holy and blameless in His sight.**" (Ephesians 1: 3-4)

Who is the Man (Puruṣa) in the Book of Ezekiel?

We have seen that this Man is not an ordinary human being. He is not an angel either. When we study chapters 40 to 47 carefully we can easily see who this Man is. Chapter 44 starts in this way: "Then the **Man** brought me back to the outer gate of the sanctuary." In the next words we read : **"The Lord said to me..."** Here we see the Man is the Lord Himself. Ezekiel, the prophet of God, accepted instructions from the Man as the word of God. Angels or human beings have no authority to measure the temple of God and set a permanent design and standard for the people of God. This Man rebuked their sinfulness and unworthiness. And also He reminded the people that the way of remission of their sin is through the offering of a blameless sacrifice. (43:23,24) In chapter 47, we read that this Man brought him to the river of the blessing of God (1-5). So there is no doubt; this Man is God Himself. At the same time He is known as Man. When we see Him closer with all the features described in the book of Ezekiel we realize He is the same **Puruṣa** as in the **Puruṣasūkta.** As we have seen earlier, in due time this **Man** came to this world with all His glory. He is the one who presently lives in us, the temple of God. The measuring rod is in His hand. He measures everything accurately. He Himself is the perfect model and permanent example for all the people of the world.

The General Revelation of God and Puruṣa

The word 'revelation' comes from the Greek word, **'apocalupto'** which means to remove the curtain or disclose. The truth of God and His way of salvation are known to us due to revelation. The love of God is the key which opens the infinite areas of the revelations of God. Jesus said that he who loves Him shall be loved by His Father, Almighty God, and He will love him and disclose Himself to him (John 14:21) He reveals His glory through the heavens and firmament

which are created by Him and He does not leave Himself without a witness in everybody's heart (Psalm 19:1; Acts 14:17)
St. Paul explains this as follows:

"For since the creation of the world God's invisible qualities- - the eternal power and divine nature - have been clearly seen, being understood from what has been made, so that men are without excuse." (Romans 1:20)

Since God reveals Himself to every one through His creation this revelation is called the General Revelation. As we have seen earlier from the **Puruṣasūkta** all these creations are the result of the **Man sacrifice.** "Through Him everything was made; without Him nothing was made." (John 1:3). His wonderful creation , the incredible universe filled with 100 billion stars of the galaxy or milky way, witness every moment to the sacrificial love of **Puruṣa**. As a child has an inborn tendency to recognize his father and mother from his birth every one of us has a place in our soul to recognize the language of the **Man - Puruṣa** - who sacrificed Himself for our creation and redemption. In the ultimate analysis **Puruṣa** is the subject and object of revelation. Therefore all revelations have to be measured by **the Man** who Himself is the measuring rod.

Word of God (Puruṣa) Is the Special Revelation

God Almighty reveals Himself through His Word. Theologians call it the special revelation. Whoever responds to the general revelation will be eligible to receive His special revelation. Without any controversy we can say the special revelation of God is His Word. St.John begins his Gospel with this opening verse: *"In the beginning was the Word, and the Word was with God, and the Word was God."* Therefore we have to understand the Word is a Person. That is the reason why he continues to write: *"He was with God in the beginning."* The third verse says that He is the reason for all creation. Then St. John says that this Word is the light of the world in darkness. From ancient times this true light of the Word was coming into the world to truth seeking people. This idea is expressed in the ninth verse: *"The true light that gives light to every man was coming into the world."* Finally quite specifically he says in verse 14: **" The Word became flesh and made His dwelling among us. . ."** Therefore, the **Man Christ Jesus** is the revealed Word of God. From the beginning He is the Word of God in heaven . The Word was creative and by that He created all the universe. When He came down to earth He was the incarnated Word who was able to redeem fallen man from sin by His eternal sacrifice.

Jesus taught his disciples that He Himself was the eternal Word. He declared, "I am the bread of life." (John 6: 35) The Pharisees could not understand His statement. Jesus explained it further: "I am the living bread that came from heaven. If any one eats this bread he will live forever. This bread is my flesh, which I will give for the life of the world." (John 6: 51) Jesus the incarnate Word was revealing the mystery of His sacrifice which is the central point of the Word of God. But even many of His disciples could not understand this and they departed Him. But Simon Peter said to Jesus, "Lord, to whom shall we go? You have the words of eternal life. (John 6: 68) At this point the disciples could understand only that He just had the words of eternal life. But after His resurrection they could clearly see that Jesus Himself was the word of life. (1 John 1: 1) About the Word, Moses wrote in the book of Deuteronomy: "It (the Word) is not up in heaven, so that you may have to ask, 'Who will ascend into heaven to get it and proclaim it to us so we may obey it?' " (Deut. 30: 12) St. Paul was very sure that this word was Christ Himself and therefore he boldly used the name Christ instead of the 'Word' when he directly quoted this passage from the Deuteronomy as follows: "Do not say in your heart, who will ascend into heaven? (that is to bring Christ down). (Romans 10: 6) Since Christ is the Word of life He Himself is the powerful Word of resurrection for by His 'shout' the dead in Christ shall rise up first and we who are still alive will be caught up together with them in the clouds with the Lord (1 Thessalonians 4:16, 17) So He is the Word of our hope and He Himself is the first and the last Word. This is very clear in Jesus' declaratioin in the book of Revelation: "I am the Alpha and Omega." (1: 8) So here is the conclusion: the revealed Word of God is Jesus Christ and He is the last Word, the final authority.

Jesus Christ Is the Measuring Rod

The main theme of the written Word of God is the Lord Jesus Christ Himself. Jesus called the Old Testament writings the written Word of God because those writings testify about Him. He said to the Jews:

> *"You diligently study the Scriptures because you think that by them you possess eternal life. These*

are the Scriptures that testify about Me..." (John 5:39).

We have already seen earlier that the main theme of the Holy Bible from the book of Genesis to the book of Revelation is the redemption of mankind through the great and eternal sacrifice of the Lord Jesus Christ. The ninth verse of the **Puruṣasūkta** from the **Ṛg Veda** also says that all the Scriptures originated because of the sacrifice of **Puruṣa.** We have discussed this idea also in chapter 14 of this book. The reason for the written Word of God is the everlasting love of God in the sacrifice of God. The very important message that God wants to communicate to the people of the world is this: "God so loved the world that He gave His one and only Son, that whoever believes in Him shall not perish but have eternal life."

Therefore, the canon of the Sacred Writings is not a set of definite rules and regulations or doctrines or human philosophy but the Man - the Lord Jesus Christ Himself. The word 'canon' is taken from the Greek and it literally means 'cane' or 'rod' of measurement. The Old Testament had been already approved by the Church fathers as the Word of God in the New Testament period. As canonical writings the twenty seven books of the New Testament from the Gospel of Matthew to the book of Revelation constitute the definite witness to Jesus Christ as Lord and Saviour and are regarded as the infallible rule of the Christian faith and life. Here, the most important criterion of canonization is the Person, Jesus Christ Himself.

Are the Vedas and the Upaniṣads the Word of God?

Now we are coming to the most important question about the **Vedas** that anybody can ask at this point. Did the Vedic sages receive revelation from God concerning the way of salvation through Jesus Christ? Do we have any prophecies about Christ besides the Hebrew Scriptures? Many Christians find difficulty in believing that Christ was revealed to the Vedic sages. If God hid the mystery of Christ from all other nations how did the wise men from the east, the Magi, come to worship Jesus at His birth in Bethlehem? They said, **"We saw His star in the east."** (Matthew 2:2) The Jewish nation had very clear revelation about Christ in their Holy Scriptures but they did not go to Bethlehem to worship Him. But the Magi were aware that Christ was worthy to receive glory and honour and worship. And they responded to the message, found Him and worshipped Him. In another context,

St. Paul, a former Jewish Rabbi, boldly asks: "**Is He the God of the Jews only?** (Romans 3:29) Was Balaam the prophet a Jew? In Numbers chapter 22 to 24 we read that the Lord talked through Balaam who was not a Jew. The Hebrew Scriptures themselves testify: "**The Lord is nigh unto them that are of a broken heart..**" (Psalms 34:29). We cannot see any indication here that the Lord is near to the broken hearted Hebrew only. He is near to everyone who comes to Him with an open heart. As it is written in the book of Romans: "**God does not show favoritism**" (Romans 2:11) The Holy Spirit testifies in the book of Jude, in the New Testament, that Enoch, the seventh from Adam, prophesied about the coming of our Lord: *"See, the Lord is coming with thousands upon thousands of His holy ones to judge everyone. . ."* (Jude: 14) Was Enoch a Jew? It is not right to believe that God reveals His plan of salvation to Jewish people only.

In the Old Testament Period itself God had the message of salvation to the people of Nineveh - the non Jewish world - but Jonah, the Hebrew prophet, was reluctant to go there and preach the message. In fact, Jonah "ran away from the Lord and headed for Tarshish." (Jonah 1:3) As Johannes Verkyl, the professor of Missiology and Evangelism at the Free University of Amsterdam, writes: "the Old Testament book of Jonah pointing to God's all embracing plans for the the Gentiles and Jonah's futile efforts to sabotage these plans." (Contemporary Missiology Page 96) However, the prophet of God had no other choice but to preach the message of deliverance. Hearing the message, all the people in the city including the king humbled themselves and repented of their sins. The Almighty God had compassion uopn them. But Jonah was greatly displeased and became angry. (Jonah 4: 1) But God asked Jonah : *Should I not be concerned about that great city (people of the city - Gentiles -).* God does not hide His message of salvation to anyone who really seeks Him. Abraham was not only the Father of Hebrews but also he was the father of many nations. God's plan was to bless every nation through Abraham. (Genesis 12: 1-3; 18: 18; 22: 18) This sovereign will of God is clearly expressed in the book of Isaiah in chapter 49.

God said to Israel: " It is too small a thing for you to be My servant to restore the tribes of Jacob and bring back those of Israel I have kept. *I will also make you a light a light for the Gentiles, that you may bring my salvation to the ends of the earth."* (Isaiah 49: 6) The nation of Israel failed to carry out this mission but from Israel herself the real Servant from the Servant's Song of Isaiah 53, Jesus Christ, came and fulfilled the eternal purpose of God. Israel made the temple of God a place of merchandise, 'a den of robbers', but Jesus entered the temple and drove out who were buying and selling there. He overturned the tables of the money changers. Proclaiming the eternal plan of God, He quoted from the Old Testament book of Isaiah (56: 7), *"My house will be called the house of prayer for ALL NATIONS."* (Mark 11: 17) Offering Himself on the cross He inaugurated the eternal way of salvation to all people of the world. From the beginning of the history of mankind Jesus was the message of salvation to the human race and God has been revealing this way to all truth-seeking people.

Who is able to say that God did not answer the prayers of the ancient sages of the East? For ages they prayed sincerely: "From darkness lead me to the light...from death lead me to immortality!" Is not Christ the answer to their prayer?

Well, from the first part of this book we see the Vedic presentation of the **Niṣkalanka Puruṣa (Sinless Man)** who was sacrificed from the foundation of the world for the redemption of all mankind. In the second part of the book we can see at least ten important characteristics of this **Puruṣa -Prajāpati's** perfect sacrifice fulfilled in the crucifixion and the resurrection of Christ. In the third part we draw near to the ultimate result of the sacrifice, **mukti** or salvation. From the **Upaniṣads** we also see the culminating result of the crucifixion and resurrection. Who is this **Puruṣa** if He is not Christ Jesus? Samuel Harrichand, a Christian Missionary, has written as follows in his booklet published in 1945: "The more I study the Vedas the greater is my love for Christ because in reading the Vedas I have discovered that Jesus Christ is the fulfillment of the Vedas." [171] Is the writing about Jesus Christ even before His birth not the revelation of God? Jesus asked the Jews:

"Is it not written in your Law, 'I have said you are gods,' to whom the word of God came - and the Scripture cannot be broken -- what about the one whom the Father set apart as His very own and sent into the world?" (John 10:34-36)

The word of God came to the people of the Old Testament. We call the sacred writings 'word of God'. Finally God Himself came down in the form of the incarnate Word. Is this glorious message expressed in human language not the word of God? No matter, whether we read it- the message of the one and the only way of salvation through the Lord Jesus Christ- from the Holy Bible or from the Vedas, are we not unmistakably aware of entering the presence of the Man of sorrows, the Puruṣa who gave His life for the sins of the world?

However, the real problem comes when we study the whole Vedic literature. Pointing out the contradictions of the Vedas, Fr. Zacharias writes:

"Do we not find therein inconsistencies, inaccuracies and even real contradictions? Do we not find in the Vedas some passages where they uphold the unity of God and other passages where the plurality of gods is clearly stated?. . . How can a literature containing these and similar other contrary views be considered as infallible and unerring when true infallibility and true inerrancy must necessarily exclude all falsehood and error."[172] Dr. Jadunatha Sinha completely agrees with him when he writes on the philosophy of the Vedas in his great work A History of Indian Philosophy. He summarizes his studies in the following sentences: "The Vedas represent different phases of religious thought. There are manifest signs of polytheism, organized polytheism, henotheism, monotheism and monism." [173]

It is true that many books are written in the Sanskrit language. People consider them as Vedic literature too. These books also consist of opinions, theories, philosophies and myths. We encounter all sorts of ideas when we go through Vedic literature. We may even see several other vedic gods named **Prajāpati** and their stories. The characters of these Prajāpatis are totally different from the divine characters of the original **Prajāpati** who is the Lord of all. As Professor Max Muller says, "**but hidden in this rubbish are precious stones.**"[174] The revelation of the true nature of God and way of salvation through the **Puruṣa** are the precious stones hidden in the whole Vedic literature.

Many Christians and many Hindus are equally excited to see the shadows of Christ, the precious Stone in the Vedas.

But some Christians do not tolerate to see Christ in the Hindu religious books. (In the same manner some Hindus do not want to see a place for Christ in their holy books.) The Christians who oppose even argue that the way of salvation in the Vedas through Jesus Christ is a counterfeit and its author is Satan because it is found in the Vedas. If Satan proclaimes the one and the only way of salvation through Jesus Christ he is destroying himself. When Jesus was accused saying He was driving out demons by the prince of demons Jesus said to them: "If Satan drives out Satan, He is divided against himself." (Matthew 12: 26) Satan never speaks the truth to anyone "for there is not truth in him." (John 8:44) It is true that Satan makes counterfeits of the original way of salvation making several other similar ways but he never says that Christ is the one and the only way of salvation. The **Puruṣa-Prajāpati** who offers Himself in sacrifice is not one among many gods of Hinduism. We cannot see Him among the gods like Rama or Krishna. This **Puruṣa-Prajāpati** represents the one and the only God who is the Lord of all creation. In fact, according to the Vedas this **Puruṣa-Prajāpati** did not perform His Self-sacrifice in this world. As we have seen in the first chapter, this sacrifice was performed in heaven in the heart of God even before the creation of the world. (See pages 55 and 59.) No one has claimed yet that this sacrifice was done on this earth or all these features were fulfilled in anybody else other than in the Lord Jesus Christ. However in chapter 2 we see that the same sacrifice came on earth by interpreting the symbol of **Aśvattha tree** - the inverted tree from heaven - and the significance of the word Puruṣa or Man. This Man was bruised and shedding blood in sacrifice in order to give heaven to sinners. The tree was completely cut off but it lived again. In this book we can see the same Jesus Christ in the New Testament who gave up His life for us in sacrifice and who rose again on the third day from the dead.

Some Hindus also feel difficulty to comprehend the message of **Puruṣasūkta** where we see the explicit way of salvation through the Lord Jesus Christ. Traditionally they were not taught in this way. The passage of **Puruṣasūkta** is clear in its presentation. Can we say Christians interpolated these passages to the **Ṛg Veda?** No! These and many other similar portions were written before the Christian era and the Vedic people preserved these writings faithfully without changing even a sound. These writings are notable for their uniqueness even though they are parallel to the Bible. And moreover, no Christian has made a serious attempt to prove that these portions of the **Ṛg Veda** communicate knowledge of Christ's sacrifice. (In this context I remember with great respect Mahakavi K.V. Simon- a well known author, Sanskrit scholar, Evangelist and a Christian leader of India, who has written briefly in few verses about this subject- **Christ and the sacrifice of Puruṣa-Prajāpati-** in his book **Vedavihāram** in 1931.)[175].

Now is God's time to communicate the gospel of Jesus to all the nations. Therefore, whenever we see the concepts of **Puruṣa-Prajāpati**'s sacrifice and the **Aśvattha Tree** which came down from heaven we glorify God for giving His eternal plan of salvation to all mankind. But we measure everything by the light of the revealed Word of God. We have the cane or the measuring rod to measure every book accurately. It is simply that the canon is the Man - **Puruṣa** - the Lord Jesus Christ. As Donald McGavran writes: "Whether we regard religious teachings and doctrines as discoveries made by men or as coloured light coming from God, Christians rejoice in whatever truth is in them, but measure it with the white light of God's revelation in Christ - the final authority."[176] The final authority and the revealed Word of God is Christ Himself. Even though we cannot consider that Vedic literature is infallible, without any doubt we can say the way of salvation through the Lord Jesus Christ was revealed to the sages of the east by God Himself. "In the past God spoke to our forefathers through the prophets at many times and in various ways, but in these last days He has spoken to us by His Son." (Hebrews 1:1-2) Remember, Christ is the Last Word.

"My Sheep recognize My Voice"

This world is filled with various voices and noises. Everybody has freedom of expression. Through voice and noise they talk. In the midst of these sounds, Jesus says, "My sheep recognize my voice." When we tune our hearts to God we recognise His voice.

> Jesus said at the time of His public ministry:
> "He (the Good Shepherd) calls his own sheep by name and leads them out. When He has brought out all His own, He goes on ahead of them, and His sheep follow Him because they know His voice. But they will never follow a stranger; in fact they will run away from him because they do not recognize a stranger's voice." (John 10:3-5)
> Jesus continued:
> "I am the good shepherd. The good shepherd lays down His life for the sheep..." (verse 11)
> Again He said:
> "I am the good shepherd; I know my sheep and My sheep know Me - just as the Father knows Me and I know the Father - and I lay down My life for the sheep." (verse 14,15) Jesus Christ was talking to the Jews who believed in Him.

Remembering all other nations of the world He continued:

"I have other sheep that are not of this sheep pen. I must bring them also. They too will listen to My voice, and there shall be one flock and one Shepherd." (verse 16)

This is the author's desire and prayer that they too listen to His voice and that is the reason why this book is written.

(Your letters to the author will help him for a revised edition of this book. Please write to him in the following address:
Joseph Padinjarekara, International Mukti Mission, 283 Homewood Ave. Willowdale, Ontario. M2R 2N6 Canada.)

I FOUND HIM THE PURUṢA

"I found Him, the Man, the Puruṣa, whom my soul loveth; I held Him and would not let Him go." (Song of Songs 3:4)
The Man said, " I will not leave you or forsake you." "I will be with you always." Jesus.

"I found Him, the Man, of whom Moses in the Law and the Prophets did write." (John 1:45)

I found Him the Man in the **Vedas and the Upaniṣads.**
The Man said, "Lo I come, in the volume of the book it is written of Me." (Ps: 40: 7)

"I sought for Him, the Man, to stand in the gap" (Ezekiel 22:30) between me and God.

I found the Man.

The Man said, "I am the way, the truth, and the life; no one comes to the Father but through Me." (John 14:6)

"For there is one God and one mediator between God and men, the Man Christ Jesus."(1.Timothy 2:5)

I found "the Man whose appearance was like bronze, with a linen cord and a measuring rod in His hand" (Ezekiel 40: 3) to measure the temple of God.

The Man said to me "You are My temple and I measure you and live there."

"I found the Man approved of God by miracles and wonders and signs". (Acts: 2:22)

I found the Man whom God ordained to judge the world.(Acts 17: 31)

He said, "He who believes in Me shall not condemned."
I found the **Puruṣa** in the **Kaṭhopaniṣad** and the **Puruṣasūkta** who is the Lord of immortality. He told me: **"Because I live you also will live."** (John 14:19)

I sang a song: "Because He lives I can face tomorrow..."

"I know the mighty **Puruṣa** of the colour of the sun beyond the darkness. Only in knowing Him does one pass over death. There is no other path leading to eternity." (**Śvetāśvataropaniṣad 3:8; Yajur Veda 31:18)**

NOTES

[1]Will Durant. "Our Oriental Heritage" (New York: Simon and Schuster (1954) Page 391.

[2] Professor Sukumar Azhicode. Tatvamasi. Third Edition (Kottayam, Kerala, India National Book Stall, 1987) Page 24. The author starts his book with this expression - the soul of the Himalayas -. He quotes a Spanish author, Juvan Scoro, who appreciateed the greatness of the Upanisads.

[3]**Ṛg Veda Sanhita,** the Sacred Hymns of the **Brāhmaṇas** (With the Commentary of Sayanacharya , Edited by F. Max Muller. Vol.VI. (Preface) London (1874).

[4] **Māndūkyopaniṣad.** Preface. Page 12. **Sriramakrishna Matham. Kerala.**

[5]An Outline of Hinduism By Fr. Zacharias O.C.D. St. Apostolic Seminary, Alwaye, Kerala. India. 1956. Page 21.

[6] Swami Prabhavananda and Frederick Manchester, The Upanishads Breath of the Eternal. New York and Scarborough (Ontario): A Mentor Book New American Library. 1975. Page 9.

[7] **Bṛhadāraṇykopaniṣad-** 1.3.28 (Commentary by Swami Mridananda) Sriramakrishna Matham, Kerala, India.

[8]Swami Nikhilananda. The Realistic Aspect of Indian Spirituality. The Indian mind. Page 242 Editor Charles a Moore (1967). East-West Center Press, University of Hawaii Press, Honolulu.

[9] "Westminister Shorter Catechism," The book of confessions of the Presbyterian Church, USA.

[10] Prātasnānamantram (A well-known prayer before bath):

> **"Pāpohaṃ pāpakarmohaṃ pāpātmā papa sambhavaḥ trāhimāṃ Pundarikaṣha sarva yajñeśvaro harih"**

[11]Shakespeare- Macbeth Act 2 Se.2 V.60

[12]Jerry Johnston "The Edge of Evil. The Rise of Satanism in North America." (Dallas, Word Publishing Dallas, 1989.) Page 11.

[13]Ibid. Page.2.

[14]**Ṛg Veda** 10:130:1

[15]Ṛg Veda 1:164:35

[16]Kaṭhopaniṣad 1.13

[17]Kaṭhopaniṣad 1.14

[18]Śathapathabrāḥmaṇa 3.1.4.3

[19] By means of sacrifice, not only men but also gods acquire immortality. **Śathapathabrāḥmaṇa.II.2.2.8-14.**"It is through sacrifice that man reaches heaven." Ibid.VIII.6.1.10.

[20]"**Ṛtam eva parameṣthi. . .**" A passage from the **Maitrāyana Saṃhita** often repeated in the **Sūtras.** See **the Gobhila Gṛhya Sūtra.2.1.7**
[21]Prajāpatir Yajñaḥ. Ṛg Veda
[22]H. Aguilar. The Sacrifice in the Ṛg Veda Page 37. (1976) Bharatiya Vidya Prakashan. Delhi. H.Aguilar quotes the verses 10.2.2.1-2 of the Śathapathabrāhmaṇa.
[23]Ṛg Veda 10:90:1-15
[24] **Māddhyandinīya Śathapathabrāḥmaṇa. VII.4:1.15.**
"**Prajāpati** is the same as Puruṣa and also same as sacrifice." Quoted from the Classical Hinduism. Page.119. By. M. Dhavamony. (Universita Gregoriana Editrice - Roma) 1982.
[25] **Kaṭhopaniṣad.3.11.**
[26]**Kaṭhopaniṣad 6:8.**
[27]**Śvetāśvataropaniṣad.3:8.** We can also see this verse in the **Yajur Veda 31:18.**
[28]H. Aguilar The Sacrifice in the Ṛg Veda. Page.68 .(Ibid).
[29]The Cross In the New Testament. By Leon Morris. Page 32.
[30]Ārshajñānam (Malayalam) by Nalappat Narayana Menon
[31] **Ṛg Veda 10: 90.1. "Atyatiṣtaddaśāngulaṃ". Vaman Shivram Apte** gives the following meaning for this his Dictionary under the word **atistha**: was over and above by 10 angulas".
The Practical Sanskrit English Dictionary. (1965) Publishers: Motilal Banarsidass, Delhi.
[32]Ārshajñānam. (Malayalam) by Nalappat Narayana Menon. Page.558. Mathrubhumi(1981.)
[33] N.J. Shende, **The Puruṣasūkta (RV 10-90) in Vedic Literature** (Publications of the Centre of Advanced Study in Sanskrit University of Poona) 1965. A four pages booklet.
[34] The Practical Sanskrit English Dictionary. (Ibid)
[35] Mariasusai Dhavamony, Classical Hinduism. Universita Gregoriana Editrice Roma (1982) Page:115.
[36] Vallathol Narayana Menon. **Ṛgvedasaṃhita.** (Page 988) Publishers: University of Kerala, India.
[37](Ibid. Page 458)
[38] Sayanacarya's Commentary on **Puruṣasūkta.** Under the first verse.
[39]Ṛg Veda 10.90.2.
[40]**Tāṇdyamahābrāḥmaṇa.** Chapter 7, Second khānda, verse 1. With the Commentary of Sayanacharya. Chaowkhamba Sanskrit Series office, Banares, India. (1935) Page 230.
[41]**Ṛg Veda 10:90.6,7.**

[42] A French author Jean L. M. translated the verse in this way in his book ,'Hymns From the Ṛg Veda.'
[43]**Ṛg Veda** 10:90.8,9.
[44]Matthew 2:3-6.
[45] **Yajurveda 32:4.**
[46]Ibid verse 5.
[47] We can see this **Śāntipātham** at the beginning of the Upaniṣads like **'Iśavāsyopaniṣad,' Bṛhadāraṇyako-paniṣad etc.**
Professor Sukumar Azhicode, one of the Sanskrit Scholars and a Hindu philosopher, even expressed that the verse is very difficult to interpret. **"Tatvamasi"** Page 191. (Malayalam.Published by N.B.S. Kerala, India.)
[48] **Sayanacarya's** Commentary on **Puruṣasūkta.** Under the verses No.7 and No.16.
[49] N.J. Shende, University of Poona. (Ibid).
[50] We have stories of incarnations like **Daśāvatāras** (10 Incarnations) in the Purāṇas. According to the **Bhāgavata Purāṇa** there were more than 10 incarnations. Almost all the scholars agree that the Puranas are written in A.D. after St. Thomas came to India and preached about the Incarnation of the Lord Jesus Christ. But before Christ we can see the shadows of the concept of incarnation in the Vedas and the Upaniṣads.
[51]**Kaṭhopaniṣad 6:1.**
[52]The Sacred Books of the Hindus. Edited by Major B.Basu. Vol.1. Page 124. Translated by various Sanskrit Scholars. 1911. Allahabad, India.
[53]Bṛhadāraṇyaka Upaniṣad 3.9.28.1
[54]Ibid.3.9.28.2
[55]The Unknown Christ of Hinduism.Raimundo Panikkar. London 1981.
[56]Ṛg Veda 10:181:2
[57]The Sacrifice in the Ṛg Veda p.90
[58]Bṛhadāraṇyaka Upaniṣad. 1.2.8.
[59]Halley's Bible Handbook.p.279. (1963)
[60]See the third characteristic of the Prajāpati-sacrifice on one of the coming pages.
[61]**Tāndyamahābrāḥmaṇa.** Chapter 7, Second khanda, verse 1. (Ibid)
[62]**Puruṣasūkta 10:90:16;** By sacrifice gods sacrificed to sacrifice. These were the earliest established principles..."**Puruṣasūkta 10:90:6.** "When the gods laid out the sacrifice with the Puruṣa as their offering...." When we study the portion carefully we understand that

without the willingness of **Puruṣa** gods cannot offer this sacrifice. Remember, the **sūkta** says that **Puruṣa** is omnipotent and the Lord of all. Therefore, we can say practically that **Puruṣa** offered Himself in this sacrifice.

[63]Leviticus 1:10.and **Māddhyndinīya Śathapathabrāhmaṇa.**

[64] **Māddhyandinīya Śathapathabrāhmaṇa.III.**

[65] **Kaṭhopaniṣad 1, 3.8.**

[66]The Christ We Adore, by Swami Ranganathananda. Page 17. American Edition 1980. (Chicago).

PART II

[67]**Kaṭhopaniṣad. 3.1**
[68]**Chāndogya Upaniṣad.**1.6:6,7.
[69]**Bṛhadāraṇyaka Upaniṣad.**1.4.1
[70]**Kātyāyana Śrautasūtram** Chapter 6 describes the rules of the animal sacrifice. Note the importance given to water and fire. It is for the purification of the animal since blameless animal is not available in this world.
[71]J. C. McRuer, The Trial of Jesus. Page.64.
[72] The Last Temptation of Christ. Its Deception and What You Should Do About It. By Erwin W.Lutzer. Page.16. Moody Press Chicago.
[73]Ibid. Page 16
[74]**Chāndogya Upaniṣad.** (Ibid)
[75]**"Anṛtād evaina varuṇān muncati." Kāthaka Saṃhita XXXI.6**
[76]**"Yathā puṣkara-palāśa apo na sliṣyante,**
evam evam-vidi pāpam karma na sliṣyata iti."
Chāndogya Upaniṣad.4.14.3.
[77]**Śathapatha brāḥmaṇa 13.6.2.2.**
[78]Richard Wurmbrand If Prison Walls could Speak. (1972. USA) Page.25.
[79]Ibid. Page 25.
[80]**Itareya Brāḥmaṇam** 2:16. Quoted from the book,' **Satyam**' (Malayalam) written by G.Suseelan.M.A.;M.A; M.A: M.A; B.Lib.Sc. B.D. (1985.)
[81] Seven Deadly Sins. By Anthony Campolo. Victor Books. 1987.
[82] Yesukristhuvinte Eliya Dāsan. (Autobiography of Pastor K. E. Abraham.) Malayalam. (1983).Pages 406-411.
[83]**Śathapatha Brāḥmaṇa XIII 1.6.3.** This verse also indicates the connection of Horse Sacrifice with Prajapati-sacrifice. - **Prajāpatirakāyata aśvamedhena. . ."**
[84]Genesis ch.22.
[85]**Śathapathabrāḥmaṇa 13.3.7.1. Tāṇdyamahābrāḥmaṇa (3.9.19.1)** also gives us a long list of the result of the sacrifice.
[86]**Ṛg Veda** 5:46.1
[87]John 18:11.
[88]**Taittirīya Saṃhita 1:3.7, 1:6.3**
Āpastamba'srauta sūtraṃ. VII.12:6.
[89]Rev. Robert J. Daly S. J. Christian Sacrifice (The Catholic University of America Press.) Page 3

[90]Sathapatha brāḥmaṇa III.7.3.1.
Quoted from the book, The Vedic and the Christian Concept of Sacrifice. Page 179. Pontifical Institute of Theology and Philosophy. Alwaye, Kerala, India.
[91] Ṛg Veda 10:90.1-15.
[92]The Cross in The New Testament. By Leon Morris. Page 5.
[93]Galatians 3:13; Deut.21:23.
[94]**Aitareya Brāḥmaṇa** II.1 **Kauṣītaki Brāhmaṇa** X.1. Quoted from' The Vedic and the Christian Concept of Sacrifice.' Page.180. (Ibid).
[95]Normal Christian Life. by Watchman Nee.
[96]See the second chapter of this book.
[97]**Itareya Brāḥmaṇa.2:6.**
[98]**Sathapatha Brāhmaṇa.7.1.2.1-11.**
[99]"The Sacrifice in the Ṛg Veda" By H. Aguilar. Page.137.
Aitareya Āraṇyaka 3,2.6.2.

[100]**Bṛhadāraṇyaka Upaniṣad. 3.9.28.4 & 5** The original verses are given below:

"Yadvṛkṣo vṛksaṇo rohati
mūlānnavataraḥ punaḥ
martyaḥ svinmṛtyuna vṛkṇaḥ
kasmānmūlāt prarohati.

Retasa iti mā vocata
jīvatastat prajāyate
dhānāruha iva vai vrkṣo-
anjasā pretya saṃbhavḥ."

(If the tree is cut off, it will live again from its root. But after the **Man (Martyaḥ)** was cut off by death, from which root does He comes forth? Do not say He is from the **ratas** (seed or semen) like a tree germinating from the seed because **ratas** comes from only the one who lives.[Remember this Man is dead.] **But the Man lives again.**)

In this verse #4, the word **Martyah** is used in the singular form. The literal meaning of **Martyaḥ** is man. Mridananda Swami translated this word as an ordinary man in this world. (**Bṛhadāraṇyaka Upaniṣad** Malayalam Commentary and translation. Publishers: Sriramakrishna matham, Kerala. 1986. page 348)

By the word **Martyaḥ** the ancient sage meant **Puruṣa** the creator of the world. This is very clear from the previous verses in the

Upaniṣad. Verses 1-3 (**Bṛhadāraṇyaka Upaniṣad** 3.9.28.1-3) deal with the **Puruṣa,** the Creator of the world and therefore the main subject of the context is the **Puruṣa** Himself.

From verse two we have already noticed that the **Puruṣa** is bruised and from His body blood was flowing. Moreover, from verse #5 we can see the **Man** is completely dead. It specifically says the Man lives again not like a tree germinating from its seed is born from the **ratas (semen).** Here the Man lives again not from the **ratas.** Therefore this man is not an ordinary human being as Mridananda Swami shows by his translation. By that wrong conception he was trying to establish the theory of re-incarnation of man.

[101] Antiquities.18:3:3. Quoted from the "Run Away World" by Michael Green.

[102] The Day Death Died. By Michael Green. Page 47. Intervarsity Press.1982.

[103] "The Day Death Died" By Michael Green. Pages.58-59.

[104] "Man Alive" by Michael Green. Page 40.

[105] John Myers, Voices From the Edge of Eternity, Spire Books, Fleming H. Revell Company, Old Tappan,
New Jersey. (1973).

[106] Ibid, Pages 23-25. John Myers compiled this narration from the biography of D. L. Moody written by A. P. Fitt. (Moody Press.).

[107] Based on the report of The Good News Weekly Vol.XI 18. May 4, 1988. (Kerala, India.)

[108] Ibid. Pages 22,23. John Myers compiled this document from the book The Contrast Between Infidelity and Christianity.

[109] **Kaṭhopaniṣad** 3:15.

[110] Church fathers' opinion about the chief-end of man. (Ibid)

[111] **Śathapathabrāhmaṇa** 5.1.1. 1-2.

[112] H. Aguilar. Ibid Page.59.

[113] Rev. Robert J.Daly. (Ibid) Page 3

.[114] A passage from the **Maitrāyana Samhita** (Ibid).

PART III

[115] Swami Nikhilananda (Ibid)
[116]**Kaṭhopaniṣad** 1:4.
[117]**Kaṭhopaniṣad** 1. 12,13.
[118]Ibid 1:20.
[119]Ibid 1.26.
[120]**Kaṭhopaniṣad** 1:12
[121] John Weldon and Zola Levitt. Is There Life After Death? Page 3
[122] Dr. Maurice S Rawlings MD Beyond Death's Door (Page 129) Bantom Book edition.
[123] Sadhu Sunder Singh Visions of the Spiritual World Pages 1,2.
[124] **Ṛg Veda** 9:113.7-11.
[125]**Ṛg Veda 4.5.5; 7.104.3.**
[126]**Kaṭhopaniṣad. 3:14.**
[127]**Kaṭhopaniṣad 2:23.**
[128]**Kaṭhopaniṣad 5.1.**
[129] The Sacred Books of the Hindus (Under **Kaṭhopaniṣad.** page 113) Edited by Major B.D. Basu, I.M.S. Allahabad, India. (1911)
[130]D. M. Datta, M.A.,PhD. The Six Ways of Knowing (University of Calcutta) 1972. Page 31.
[131]Kaṭhopaniṣad 3:3.
[132]Ibid 3.4
[133] **Bṛhadāraṇykopaniṣad 1.5.3.**
[134]**Kaṭhopaniṣad** 3:11; 6:8.
[135] Jadunath Sinha, M.A., Ph.D. A History of Indian Philosophy, 2 Volumes. (1952). Central Book Agency
14. Bankim Chatterjee Street. Calcutta.
[136] Ibid. page 31. **Sāmkhyatattvārthakaumudi.**6.
[137] Ibid Vol.2. Pages 33,34.
[138] Swami Ranganathananda, The Message of the Upaniṣads. See page 526. Bharatiya Vidya Bhavan, Bombay 7. (1985).
Swami Prabhavananda The Upaniṣads Breath of the Eternal A Mentor Book, New American Library, New York.(1975)
[139] V. S. Apte, The Practical Sanskrit English Dictionary. (Revised Enlarged Edition.1965). Motilal Banarsidass, Bangalow Road, Javaharnagar, Delhi 7.
[140] **Advayatārakopaniṣad.**16.
[141]**Gurugīta** 44th verse.

[142] **Advayatārakopaniṣad** 17,18.
[143] **Bṛhadāranykopaniṣad** 1:3.28.
[144]**Gurugīta 1:79.**
[145] **Iśavasyopaniṣad** verse 11.
"avidyayā mṛtyuṃ tīrtvā vidyayā amṛtamaśnute"
[146] Jawaharlal Nehru. The Discovery of India. (Page 53.) 1946. The Signet Press, Calcutta.
[147]**Śvetāśvataropaniṣad** 3:8.; **Yajurveda** 31:18.
[148] At the end of the **Puruṣasūkta** in the commentary part. Quoted by Sayanacharya.
[149] M. Dhavamony, Ibid Page 468.
[150] M. Dhavamony, Ibid. **Śathapathabrāhmaṇa** 3.6.2.16.
[151] Acharya Daya Prakash Titus, Fulfillment of Vedic Quest in the Lord Jesus Christ. Page 21. (Published by the author. India).
[152]Ibid, Page 22.
[153] Dr. P.J. Titus. Karma and the Cross. (From **Mukti Bimonthly**, Vol.2.No.1. September 1983.) Ontario, Canada. This article was originally published in the periodical, **Cross and Crown**, Udayapur, India.
[154] Ibid.
[155] The Mahābhārata. Śāntiparva
[156] Pat Means The Mystical Maze Information from the back cover. (Campus Crusade for Christ.) (1976)
[157] Josh McDowell, From the Foreword of The Mystical Maze (Ibid).
[158] The Mystical Maze (Ibid). Page 131.
[159]From **Maclean's** (Canada's Weekly News Magazine, Toronto, March 26, 1990.) This article appears various news medias of America. In this article the Governments are invited to contact: Maharishi World Capital of the Age of Enlightenment, Maharishi Nagar 201 304, U.P, India.
[160] Maharishi Mahesh Yogi, Maharishi's Master Plan to Create Heaven on Earth (Reconstruction of the Whole World.) Taken from the summary of the book from the **Maclean's** (March 26, 1990.)
[161] This author's friend was advised to go for **Yoga** treatment when he was admitted in the Mount Sinai Hospital in Toronto.
[162]Pat Means (Ibid) Page 137.
[163] Ibid Page 140.
[164] Ibid, Page 140.
[165] Maharishi Mahesh Yogi, Meditations of Maharishi. Pages 177,178.
[166] James S.Stewart,D.D. A Man In Christ (1935).
[167] Kaṭhopaniṣad 3:14, (Ibid) Ephesians 5:14.

[168] Swami Nikhilananda , Hinduism Its Meaning for the Liberation of Spirit. (Page 108) Sri Ramakrishna Math, Mylapore, Madras 4. India.(1968).
[169] Ibid. Page 104.
[170] Ibid.
[171] Samuel Harrichand, Illumination of Ideas of India. (Printed at the Labour Advocate 61, Hadfield St. Georgetown, British Guiana. (1945).
[172] Fr.Zacharias , O.C.D. (Ibid) Page 56.
[173] Dr. Jadunath Sinha. Ibid. Page 1.
[174] Illumination of Ideas of India. (Ibid) quoted from page 8.
[175] Vedavihāram Mahakavi K.V. Simon. (Chapter 3. verses 328 to 344. Pages 26,27). C.M.S Press Kottayam. (1931)
[176] Donald Mc Gavran, The Clash Between Christianity and Cultures. (1974) Page 8. Canon Press, Washington.

BIBLIOGRAPHY

Sanskrit Texts

(1) **Bṛhadāraṇyokopaniṣad** (With Malayalam Commentary by Mṛdananda Swami) Sriramakrisna matham, Puranatukara 680 551, Trichur, Kerala, India. (1986)

(2) **Chāndogyopaniṣad** (With Malayalam Commentary by Mṛdānanda Swami) Sriramakrisna matham, Puranatukara 680 551, Trichur, Kerala, India. (1982)

(3) **Īśavāsyopaniṣad** (With English translation. Edited by Major B.D. Basu.) Title: The Sacred Books of the Hindus. The Panini Office, Bhuveneswari Asrama Bahadurgang, Allahabad, India. (1911)

(4) **Īśavāsyopanisad** (With Malayalam Commentary by Mṛdānanda Swami) Sriramakrishna matham Puranatukara 680 551, Trichur, Kerala, India. (1986)

(5) **Kaṭhopaniṣad** (With Malayalam Commentary by Mṛdānanda Swami) Sriramakrishna matham Puranatukara 680 551, Trichur, Kerala India. (1984)

(6) **Kaṭhopaniṣad** (With English translation. Edited by Major B. D. Basu. Title: The Sacred Books of the Hindus, India (1911)

(7) **Kātyāyana Śrautasūtra** (English Translation). By H. G. Ranade, M.A; PhD. S. M. S Letter Press, 129/2 Erandavane, Poone 411004 India. (1978)

(8) **Māndukyopaniṣad** (With Malayalam Commentary by Mṛdānanda Swami). Sriramakrishna matham, Puranatukara, Trichur. Kerala, India (1984)

(9)**Puruṣasūktam** (Portions from the **Ṛg Veda** 10: 90: 1-16 with Sayanacharya's Commentary written in Sanskrit.) **Ānandaśrama Samskṛta granthāvali**, Ānandaśramamudrānalayam, India.

(10) **Puruṣasūktam** (Portions from the **Ṛg Veda** 10: 90: 1-16 with Hindi translation by Shri Daulatarama Shasti Gouda.) The Chowkhamba Sanskrit Series Office, P.O. Box 8, Varanasi (1963)

(11) **Puruṣasūktam** (**Ṛg Veda** 10:90: 1-16. With English translation by Arthur A. Macdonell. Title: A Vedic Reader For Students.) Oxford University Press. England. (1917)

(12) **Ṛg Veda Saṃhita** The Sacred Hymns of the Brāhmaṇas. (English translation). Together with the Commentary of Sayanacharya. Edited by F. Max Muller. W. M. H. Allen and Co. 13

Waterloo Place, SW, London.(1874)

(13) **Ṛg Veda Saṃhita** (Malayalam translation by Vallathol Narayana Menon. University of Kerala, India.)
(14) **Śathapathabrāḥmaṇa** (Śuklayajurvedantargata Māddhyandīniya Śathapathabrāḥmaṇa) Edited by Vedaviśārada Mīmāmsa Kesari, Pandit A. Chinnaswami Shastry Pandit Pattābhīra Shastry and Pandit Ramanatha Dikṣita. Oriental Cultural Literature. Chaukhambha, P.O. Box 139. Jadu Bhavan, K 37/116, Gopal Mandir Lane. Varanasi 221001. India. (1984)
(15) **Śathapathabrāḥmaṇa** (With English translation by Max Muller. Title: Sacred Books of the East Vol. XLIV, XI, XII, XIII. Oxford at Clarendon Press. (1900)
(16) **Śvetāśvataropaniṣad** (With Malayalam commentary by Mṛdānanda Swami) Sriramakrishna matham, Puranatukara, Trichur. (1984)
(17) **Tāṇdyamahābrāḥmaṇa** (With Sayanacharya's Commentary in Sanskrit.) The Chawkhamba Sanskrit Series, Benares, India (1935).
(18) **Vajasaneyi Mādhyandīna Śukla Yajurveda Saṃhita** Edited by Pandit Jagdishlal Shasti. Motilal Banarsidass, Delhi. (1971)

Malayalam Books

(19) Abraham K. E. (Pastor) Yeshukristuvinte Eliya Dasan (Autobiography). Hebron, Kumbanad, Kerala, India.
(20) Azhikode Sukumar. (Professor) Tatvamasi. N.B.S. Kottayam, Kerala, India. (1987)
(21) Nalappat Narayana Menon Ārshajñānam Mathrubhumi Press, Calicut 1 , Kerala, India. (1981)
(22) Simon K.V. Mahakavi. Vedavihāram C.M.S Press Kottayam Kerala, India. (1931).
(23) G. Suseelan M.A., M.A., M.A., M.A., B.Lib.Sc., B.D. Satyam (1985)
(24) G.Suseelan M.A., M.A., M.A., M.A., B.Lib.Sc. B.D.Sanātanaguru (1984). Both books published by Pravachana Pradeepika Publications, Aramada, P.O. Trivandrum 32. Kerala, India.

English Books:

(25) Aguilar H. The Sacrifice in the Ṛg Veda Bharatiya Vidya Prakasam Delhi, India. (1976)

(26) Campolo Anthony, Seven Deadly Sins Victor Books, A division of SP Publications, Inc. Wheaton, Illinois 60187 U.S.A. (1987).

(27) Rev. Daly Robert J. S. J. Christian Sacrifice Catholic University of America Press, Washington, (1978).

(28) Dr. Datta D. M. M.A.,PhD. Six Ways of Knowing, University of Calcutta. (1972.)

(29) Dhavamony Mariasusai, Classical Hinduism, Universita Gregoriana Editrice Roma (1982).

(30) Durant Will, Our Oriental Heritage, Simon and Schuster, New York. (1954).

(31) Green Michael, The Day Death Died, Interversity Press. U.S.A. (1982)

(32) Green Michael, Man Alive, U.S.A.

(33) Harrichand Samuel, Illumination of Ideas of India, Georgetown, British Guiana. (1945).

(34) Johnston Jerry, The Edge of Evil, The Rise of Satanism in North America, Word Publishing, Dallas, (1989).

(35) Lutzer Erwin W. The Last Temptation of Christ, Its Deception and What You Should Do about It. Moody Press, Chicago.

(36) McGavran Donald, The Clash Between Christianity and Cultures, Canon Press, Washington. (1974).

(37) Means Pat, The Mystical Maze, Campus Crusade for Christ, U.S.A. (1976)

(38) Morris Leon, Cross In the New Testament.

(39) Myers John, Voice From the Edge of Eternity, Spire Books, Fleming H. Revell Company, Old Tappan, New Jersey. (1973).

(40) Nehru Jawaharlal, The Discovery of India, The Signet Press, Calcutta. (1946)

(41) Nikhilananda Swami, The Realistic Aspect of Indian Spirituality, The Indian Mind, (Edited by Charles A. Moore, East West Centre Press, University of Hawaii Press, Honolulu.(1967).

(42) Nikhilananda Swami, Hinduism Its Meaning for the Liberation of Spirit, Shriramakrishna Math, Mylapore, Madras. (1968).

(43) Panikkar Raimundo, The Unknown Christ of Hinduism, London (1981).

(44) Prabhavananda Swami The Upanishads Breath of the Eterna New American Library, New York. (1975).

(45) Ranganathananda Swami The Christ We Adore, Chicago. (1980)

(46) Ranganathananda Swami The Message of the Upanisads Bharatiya Vidya Bhavan, Bombay. (1985).

(47) Rawlings Maurice S. M.D. Beyond Death's Door, Banton, U.S.A (1979).
(48) Shakespeare, Macbeth
(49) Dr. Sinha Jadunath M.A. PhD. A History of Indian Philosophy, Two Volumes. Central Book Agency, 14 Bankim Chatterjee Street, Calcutta. (1952).
(50) Stewart James D. D. A Man In Christ (U.S.A) (1935).
(51) Fr. Thachil Jose, The Vedic And Christian Concept of Sacrifice Pontifical Institute of Theology and Philosophy, Alwaye 683 103, Kerala, India. (1985).
(52) Acharya Daya Prakash Titus, Fulfillment of Vedic Quest in the Lord Jesus Christ, (India),
(53) Verkuyl Johannes, Contemporary Missiology William B. Eerdmans Publishing Company, Grand Rapidds, Michigan.(1978)
(54) Watchman Nee Normal Christian Life, GLS Bombay.
(55) Wurmbrand Richard, If Prison Walls Could Speak, (U.S.A) (1972).
(56) Fr. Zacharias O.C.D. An Outline of Hinduism St. Apostolic Seminary, Alwaye, Kerala, India. (1956).

Sanskrit English Dictionaries:

V. S. Apte's Sanskrit English Dictionary (Revised Enlarged Edition), Motilal Banarsidass, Bangalow Road, Jawaharnagar, Delhi. (1965).
Sir Monier Williams A Sanskrit English Dictionary (New Edition, greatly enlarged and improved). Delhi. (1974).

The Holy Bible

King James Version.

New American Standard Version.

New International Version.